# THE EARLY GERMANS

# THE
# EARLY GERMANS

by

## E. A. THOMPSON

CLARENDON PRESS · OXFORD
1965

*Oxford University Press, Amen House, London E.C.4*

GLASGOW NEW YORK TORONTO MELBOURNE WELLINGTON
BOMBAY CALCUTTA MADRAS KARACHI LAHORE DACCA
CAPE TOWN SALISBURY NAIROBI IBADAN ACCRA
KUALA LUMPUR HONG KONG

PRINTED IN GREAT BRITAIN BY ROBERT MACLEHOSE AND CO. LTD
THE UNIVERSITY PRESS, GLASGOW

# PREFACE

THIS account of early Germanic society is intended for readers of the relevant chapters of Caesar and Tacitus. My intention has been to discuss concisely some of the major problems raised by these great authorities. In the first two chapters there are but few references to the Roman government: Germanic society is considered for the most part as though it had existed in a political vacuum. In Chapter Three, therefore, an attempt is made to show, mainly on the basis of evidence given by Tacitus in his *Histories* and *Annals*, how the Romans contrived in some ways to distort the development of Germanic society so as to serve the interests of peace and property on the Imperial frontier. And finally there is a chapter on warfare, the subject on which we are best informed. In this I have not confined myself to the times of Caesar and Tacitus, but for the sake of completeness have taken in the whole Roman period down to the sixth century A.D. But I have not included any systematic account of the Roman campaigns across the Rhine and the Danube, for these have been brilliantly narrated by Sir Ronald Syme in the *Cambridge Ancient History*.

The modern literature on early Germany is mountainous. I have read only a fraction of it, and have referred in the footnotes only to a fraction of what I have read. There are as many views of early German social history as there are scholars who have written about it. I have put down somewhat dogmatically what seems to me the most probable way of interpreting the various pieces of evidence; but what I have written is merely a personal view, and its purpose is no more than to provoke the reader into forming opinions of his own on the various questions that arise.

In the footnotes reference is made not only to Caesar, Tacitus, Dio Cassius, and other writers who speak directly of our period, but also to authors of much later centuries—Ammianus Marcellinus, Procopius, even Adam of Bremen. The reason for this is that these historians sometimes provide parallels to what is said by Caesar, Tacitus, etc., and therefore increase our confidence in them; and sometimes they show that phenomena observed by the earlier authors survived here and there into later ages. But it must be emphasized that Ammianus and other late writers prove nothing for the period of Caesar and Tacitus. The fact that an institution or the like is attested by Ammianus as existing among the Alamanni or the Visigoths in the fourth century A.D. by no means shows that it existed also among the Germans of whom Tacitus speaks. The point is an elementary one, but it has frequently been disregarded in the past by those German scholars who are not content to admit that our knowledge of the early history of their country is sparse and shadowy.

It is necessary nowadays for any writer on the early Germans to state, however briefly, what value he attaches to the works of Caesar and Tacitus. It is hard to resist the impression that E. Norden's splendid book *Die germanische Urgeschichte und Tacitus Germania* has had a calamitous effect on the subsequent study of primitive Germany by Continental scholars. In the Preface to his second edition Norden himself was obliged to protest— vainly, as it turned out—against the use to which his ideas were being put. As the years go by, less and less credence has been given to the works of our two major authorities, and more and more of their assertions are written off as mere echoes of that tradition of Greek ethnographical writing which Norden did so much to illumine. If Caesar and Tacitus alike stress the chastity of the early Germans, this is irrefragable proof, we are told, not that the early Germans were chaste by Roman standards but that the two authors were following a common source. Who was this common authority? The figure of Poseidonius dominates the landscape. Caesar and Tacitus pillaged his work ruthlessly. We can hardly deny that Caesar did in fact come in contact with the Germans during his campaigns in Gaul. But he threw away his great opportunity: his ethnological chapters on the Germans are not based on what he saw himself, but on somewhat unskilful use of the observations of Poseidonius and other earlier writers. If he had not had access to these authors his ignorance could hardly have been more complete.

By such argumentation, which is exceedingly widespread, I have not been convinced; and in general I accept the uncommon view that the explicit assertions of Caesar and Tacitus are credible unless they are self-evidently erroneous (which they rarely are) or unless there is archaeological or other evidence (and there rarely is) with which they cannot reasonably be reconciled.

The reader will no doubt have J. G. Anderson's edition of Tacitus' *Germania* (Oxford, 1938) at his side. It is of great value as an introduction to the subject. I wish especially to acknowledge my indebtedness to the two fine books of H. M. Chadwick, *The Origin of the English Nation* (Cambridge, 1907) and *The Heroic Age* (Cambridge, 1912). I differ from his conclusions in a number of ways. But he asked the right questions, and none can fail to admire the vast knowledge he brought to bear upon his subject, his lucid exposition, and the historical method he used in tackling the problems.

Chapter Four appeared originally in *Past and Present*, xiv (1958). I am grateful to the Editor of that journal for allowing its re-publication here, with some minor changes.

# CONTENTS

# ABBREVIATIONS

*AE*: *L'année épigraphique.*

Amm. Marc.: Ammianus Marcellinus, ed. C. U. Clark (Berlin, 1910–15).

*Chronica Minora*: T. Mommsen, *Chronica Minora saec. iv. v. vi. vii* MGH. Auctores Antiquissimi, vols. ix, xi, xii (Berlin, 1892–8).

*Cod. Euric.*: *Legum codicis Euriciani fragmenta*: see s.v. *Legg. Visig.* Euric was king of the Visigoths in Gaul from 466 to 484.

Dessau: H. Dessau, *Inscriptiones Latinae Selectae*, reprinted (Berlin, 1954–5).

Greg. Tur., *HF*: Gregory of Tours, *History of the Franks*, ed. B. Krusch and W. Levison (*MGH, Scriptores rerum Merovingicarum*, Hanover, 1951).

Jacoby: F. Jacoby, *Die Fragmente der griechischen Historiker*, Zweiter Teil (Berlin, 1926–30).

*Legg. Burg.*: *Leges Burgundionum*, ed. L. R. de Salis (Hanover, 1892).

*Legg. Visig.*: *Leges Visigothorum*, ed. K. Zeumer (Hanover, 1902), including Euric's code on pp. 3–32.

*MGH*: *Monumenta Germaniae Historica*, ed. G. H. Pertz, T. Mommsen, and others (Hanover, 1826 ff.).

Migne, *PL*: J. P. Migne, *Patrologiae cursus completus: series Latina* (Paris, 1844 ff.).

P.-W.: Pauly-Wissowa-Kroll's *Real-Encyclopädie der classischen Altertumswissenschaft.*

Paul. Diac.: Paulus Diaconus, *Historia Langobardorum*, ed. G. Waitz (Hanover, 1878).

*SHA*: *Scriptores Historiae Augustae*, ed. D. Magie (Loeb Series, London, 1930–2).

The *History* of Agathias, together with the fragments of Eunapius and Peter the Patrician, will be found in L. Dindorf, *Historici Graeci Minores*, 2 vols. (Leipzig, 1871).

# CHAPTER ONE

# THE GERMANS IN THE TIME
# OF JULIUS CAESAR

IN the year 12 B.C. the Roman armies on the Rhine began a general offensive against western Germany. After four years of dangerous fighting and more than one escape from disaster they had reached the Elbe. They maintained themselves precariously in the lands which they had overrun until A.D. 9, when Quintilius Varus and his three legions were destroyed, and the Emperor Augustus' occupation of Germany came substantially to an end.

Julius Caesar's *Memoirs of the Gallic War*, published in 51 B.C., give us a glimpse of Germany at the very moment when the Romans reached it; while Tacitus' monograph on Germany appeared in A.D. 98, long after the Imperial forces had been expelled. It was Caesar himself who brought the Romans to the Rhine in force, so that the Germanic society which he observed had hitherto been almost wholly free from direct Roman influence. But Tacitus describes Germanic society as it had become when Roman civilization had long been established on its western and southern borders, and contact between Germany and the Empire had for many years been direct and unbroken.

Now it is hardly credible that the native society can have been left unaffected by events of such magnitude as the arrival of Roman civilization on the Rhine and the Danube and the temporary extension of Roman power to the Elbe. No doubt Germanic society in Caesar's day was not static: it would have changed and developed, to be sure, in the normal course of events even if the Romans had never crossed the Alps. But the process of development must unquestionably have been affected by the conquest and above all by the continued presence of Roman civilization on the frontiers of Germany. It is in no way surprising, then, that the social life of the Germans which Tacitus described was in many ways different from what Caesar had seen 150 years earlier. We cannot simply assume that where the two accounts differ the later writer is 'correcting' the earlier. Still less can we stoop to the device of altering Tacitus' text so as to bring his description into line with Caesar's. Nor is there any evidence for supposing that, whereas Caesar is describing abnormal conditions—the peoples whom he had in mind were, or had recently been, in a state of migration—Tacitus discusses what was the normal state of affairs in Germany in Caesar's time as well as in his own. The underlying cause of these and similar errors of method is the assumption that societies do not change or at any rate that Germanic society could not have changed very much in the century and a half which separated our two great authorities. On the contrary, we should be in the presence of an historical problem of the first order if no significant change had been brought about by the penetration into Germany of the officials, legionaries, traders, and the ideas, of the Romans.

What then was Germanic society like when it had not yet been seriously affected by Mediterranean civilization? What was its nature when Caesar bridged the Rhine in 55 B.C. and burned the empty villages and the deserted cornlands of the Sugambri? And how and why did that society change in the four or five restless generations that followed?

## 1. Material Civilization

In the middle of the first century B.C. the Germanic peoples living east of the Rhine were primarily pastoralists,[1] but they were not nomadic pastoralists. They did not drive their flocks and herds northwards in springtime and southwards in the autumn, following the green grass, like the nomads of the Eurasian steppe. In moist and forested Germany the vegetation was not so strictly seasonal as to force the inhabitants into the ways of nomads. The life of the early German was not entirely dependent upon, and conditioned by, his possession of flocks and herds. No doubt these were his principle means of subsistence. These together with hunting supplied him with the greater part of his foodstuffs— meat, milk, cheese.[2] These formed his chief source of wealth and dignity. Yet the care of his flocks and herds was not the sole occupation of his peacetime life. The Romans knew that, although some Germanic peoples resembled the nomads in certain ways, the Germans were nonetheless distinct from the nomads.[3]

Their cattle were stunted and puny in contrast with the enormous oxen which ran wild in the forests, for 'the more completely the ox was tamed and deprived of its natural food, the more drastically, under primitive conditions of farming, it diminished in size'.[4] In the opinion of the Romans their horses, too, were not remarkable either for beauty or for speed, though daily training

---

[1] Caesar, *BG* vi. 22. 1, 29. 1.

[2] Ibid., iv. 1. 8, vi. 22. 1; Poseidonius, 87 F 22 (Jacoby); Pomponius Mela, iii. 3; cf. Strabo, vii. 1. 3.

[3] Strabo, loc. cit.; Tacitus, *G* xlvi. 2. At the beginning of his account of the Franks, Agathias, *Hist.* i. 2, is careful to say: εἰσὶ γὰρ οἱ Φράγγοι οὐ νομάδες, ὥσπερ ἀμέλει ἔνιοι τῶν βαρβάρων, κτλ.

[4] J. G. D. Clark, *Prehistoric Europe: The Economic Basis* (London, 1952), 123; cf. Tacitus, *G* v. 1 f., *A* iv. 72. 3; Agathias, *Hist.* i. 4, p. 146 Dindorf.

could make something of them.[1] It is true that German warriors serving in the Roman army would sometimes be allowed to retain their own unsaddled horses as well as their own inferior weapons.[2] Yet Caesar found it noteworthy that they did not import horses from abroad; and he thought it advisable on one occasion during his wars in Gaul to supply Roman horses to some Germanic cavalrymen whom he had enlisted from beyond the Rhine.[3] Even their livestock, then, the very basis of the Germans' economy, was of inferior quality by Roman standards.

But if the Germans were pastoralists in the first place, their primitive agriculture was by no means negligible, though its importance will have varied from place to place according to local conditions. True, Caesar insists on the subordinate part which it played in the German economy (p. 3 n. 1 above), and he points out that grain was a comparatively small item in the diet of at least the Suebi.[4] But he finds occasion to mention specifically the agriculture of several Germanic peoples;[5] and in the first century A.D. one exceptionally advanced people, the Ubii, practised a method of fertilizing their fields which was akin to marling.[6] Although Tacitus believed that the Germans grew corn crops only, a wide variety of root-crops and vegetables was in fact known to

[1] Caesar, *BG* iv. 2. 2; Tacitus, *G* vi. 3: see p. 117 n. 1 below.
[2] Id., *H* iv. 12 *fin.*
[3] Caesar, loc. cit.; cf. vii. 65. 5; Orosius, vii. 34. 5; Zosimus, iv. 22. 1–3.
[4] *BG* iv. 1. 8. But a century later Pliny, *NH* xviii. 149, mentions oat-meal porridge as eaten in Germany; cf. Tacitus, *G* xvi. 4 *frugibus.*
[5] *BG* iv. 1. 2 (Usipetes and Tencteri), 7 (Suebi), 19. 1 (Sugambri). On German agriculture note also iv. 1. 6; Tacitus, *G* xv. 1, xlv. 4, *A* xiii. 54. 3; Dio Cassius, lxxi. 20. 1; Herodian, vii. 2. 3; Claudian, *i cons. Stil.* 222 ff.; etc. On its importance see further A. Dopsch in W. Reeb, *Tacitus Germania* (Leipzig and Berlin, 1930), 152 § 4.
[6] Pliny, *NH* xvii. 47; cf. 43; Varro, *RR* i. 7. 8; cf. on the relatively advanced Ubii Caesar, *BG* iv. 3. 3.

them;[1] and if a more fertile tract of land than their own were found to be lying empty or weakly defended beyond their frontier, a whole people might be expected to migrate into it and build their rude homes there. The Romans believed that this longing for richer land explained the unending pressure of the forest- and marsh-dwelling Germans on the cleared and fertile fields of Gaul.[2] In fact, Caesar himself admits that if a Germanic people were prevented by the raids of a more powerful neighbour from sowing and reaping their crops for a sufficient time, they would have to move away from their homes altogether to some place of greater safety (p. 27 n. 3 below). Their agriculture was no mere digging-stick gardening: even the Bronze-Age rock carvings at Bohuslän in southern Sweden include a picture of an ox-drawn plough.[3] In a word, although crop-raising was subordinate to stock-breeding, it was nevertheless an essential and indispensable part of the Germanic economy.

In Caesar's day the Germans were ardent hunters, and the enthusiasm which they brought to this occupation does not prove that they hunted for sport only. They did so of necessity, and the game which they took formed an integral part of their food supply and provided them with some of their clothing.[4] They were also food-gatherers to the extent that they collected and ate wild fruits and berries as a staple part of their diet;[5] for

---

[1] Tacitus, *G* xxvi. 2. For a complete list of their crops see J. Hoops, *Waldbäume und Kulturpflanzen im germanischen Altertum* (Strasbourg, 1905).

[2] Caesar, *BG* i. 28. 4 (cf. Strabo, iv. 3. 3 *fin.*), 31. 5, and 11, ii. 4. 1; Tacitus, *H* iv. 73; but note id., *G* v. 1 *satis ferax*; Pliny, *NH* xvii. 26.

[3] Hoops, op. cit. 499–508; cf. Tacitus, *G* xviii. 4 *iuncti boves*.

[4] Caesar, *BG* iv. 1. 8, vi. 21. 3; Seneca, *Dial.* i. 4. 14; Tacitus, *G* xvii. 2, xxiii. 1; *Paneg. Lat.* xii (ix). 24. 2. I see no contradiction between Caesar, *BG* iv. 1. 8, and Tacitus, *G* xv. 1: see p. 51 n. 3 below.

[5] Ibid., xxiii. 1.

with the exception of the apple they did not cultivate fruit-trees in Caesar's time.[1] In the days of Tacitus they may have begun to cultivate them, as they saw the Romans do across the Rhine,[2] and later still they certainly grew them in Roman territories which they overran and occupied: they then inherited the fruit orchards which the Romans had planted, and they learned to tend them.[3]

The Iron Age had begun among the Germans several centuries before the time of Julius Caesar, but their use of iron was severely limited, at any rate by Roman standards, even at the end of the first century A.D. (p. 111 below); and it is not until the fourth century that we hear of the Romans exacting an indemnity of iron from a Germanic people whom they had defeated in war.[4] Metal of any kind was no doubt a luxury material for domestic utensils, most of which were made either of wood or leather by the menfolk or of clay by the women. Of the larger metal objects used by the Germans, apart from their weapons, most were made of bronze: the bronze industry, though not a bronze arms industry, continued to flourish throughout the Iron Age in western Germany. In the case of many handicrafts technical skill was as high beyond the Roman frontier as it was within it; but the quantities of raw materials, such as iron, which were at the disposal of Roman craftsmen were almost infinitely higher than those available to the northern barbarians.

---

[1] Ibid., v. 1, xxvi. 2; Varro, loc. cit. On the apple see Hoops, op.cit. 476–81.

[2] Ibid., 534 f.

[3] See e. g. K. Bertsch, 'Die Obstreste aus den Alamannengräbern von Oberflacht', *Berichten d. deutschen botanischen Gesellschaft*, xlv (1927), 23–30; cf. Claudian, *In Eutrop.* ii. 197.

[4] Libanius, *Or.* xviii. 78.

The bulk of their pottery was made by hand, and pieces turned on the wheel were distinctly unusual. The Germans could use the wheel, but they could not employ it extensively and systematically because of the rarity of large centres of population among them. Only an occasional itinerant potter would make his way from community to community selling wheelmade pots designed for the special needs of the purchasers.[1] Hand-made pottery was predominant, and this in itself suggests a very low level of material civilization in the communities which used it.

Finally, there is no certain evidence that the Germans of the times of Caesar and Tacitus could write. Even if the notorious *notae* mentioned by Tacitus[2] were a form of runes it still remains the case that these runes were, so far as can be told, nothing but a kind of private and personal code which was used only in connexion with the casting of lots. Now many Germans learned to speak Latin as a result of living among the Romans as hostages or as mercenary soldiers; and the letters which were sent from time to time by Germanic chieftains to the Romans were written in Latin. But it does not follow that they were written by Germans: they were probably written for them by Roman war-prisoners or Roman traders or in later days by Christian priests.[3]

The Germans of Caesar's time, then, were primarily stock-breeders, although their crop-raising was an indispensable part of their economy. Hunting and food-

[1] This may perhaps be inferred from R. von Uslar, *Westgermanische Bodenfunde d. ersten bis dritten Jahrhunderts* (Berlin, 1938), 9, 11, 83 f.; id., *Germania*, xix (1935), 254. Note also ibid. xv (1931), 101, for what seems to be the workshop of a wheel-using potter.

[2] *G* x. 1. The case for dating the invention of runes to the pre-Roman period has not in my opinion been made out.

[3] Tacitus, *A* ii. 63. 1, 88. 1; Dio Cassius, lxviii. 8. 1; Amm. Marc. xxix. 4. 7, xxxi. 15. 5; John Chrysostom, *Ep.* xiv.

gathering were still necessary tasks. They had some, but not much, iron at their disposal. They used handmade pottery almost universally; and they were pre-literate.

## 2. Social Organization

Differences of wealth among any one Germanic people were slight in Julius Caesar's time, and the private ownership of land was still unknown. Each year the leading men or 'magistrates', as Caesar calls them for want of a better term, would decide which parts of the people's land were to be brought under the plough. They would then allocate these selected parts to the various clans and would settle the extent and site of each clan's holding, leaving the area tilled in the previous year to lie fallow.[1] When they received their allotment the clansmen would plough the land with their ox-drawn ploughs, and reap their harvests; and they did so in common without dividing up the allotment among the various individuals or households included in the clan, and hence they must also have appropriated the fruits of the land in common.[2] The fact is that when the means of subsistence were continuously re-distributed substantial inequalities in the standard of living could hardly arise, and there were few ways in which the leading men could monopolize resources for their own private use. The annual re-allocation of the arable among the German clans would tend to maintain the equality of the different clans' wealth in so far as their

[1] Caesar, *BG* vi. 22. 2 (where *principes*, I think, explains *magistratus*). His words do not imply an annual migration of the whole community, a type of economy which had died out of most parts of Europe in Neolithic times: Clark, op. cit. 92 f.

[2] Caesar, *BG* iv. 1. 7 'privati ac separati agri apud eos (sc. Suebos) nihil est', vi. 22. 2 'neque quisquam agri modum certum aut finis habet proprios' (of the Germans in general).

wealth was derived from crops at all. On the other hand, although the pastures were unenclosed and common to everyone, we may assume that the herds were held on an individual basis,[1] for it is difficult to believe that cattle acquired as plunder were always owned collectively by the plunderers. This might be the case if the plundering party was composed of the warriors of a single clan; but in fact there were other kinds of raiding bands which would not have owned their booty collectively (p. 48 f. below). It follows that there were differences of wealth in Caesar's Germany, however slight these differences may have been—and in fact they *were* slight, as Caesar clearly implies.[2]

Caesar's comment on the Germanic peoples' system of land-tenure deserves the most careful notice. He is aware of the social consequences which would have resulted had private ownership of land developed fully among them. In extending the area of their property the more influential landowners, if they had existed, would have expropriated the humbler. The accumulation of privately owned wealth would have given rise to class struggles, which he implies were not to be found among the Germans of his time. Wide differences of wealth would have led to tension between the leading men and the common warriors, tension which, as things were, did not exist, for in the actual conditions observed by him each warrior could see that his own wealth,

[1] This is not proved, however, by *BG* vi. 35. 6 'magno pecoris numero, cuius sunt cupidissimi barbari', for clans can be as greedy as individuals for cattle. Moreover, if we say that the individual 'owned' the cattle, are we to suppose that he owned them in his own right, or as the head of an extensive family, or as a clan chief, or as representing the community in some way? Could he, for example, sell cattle without reference to any of his followers? Little can be made in this connexion of the document printed in V. Arangio-Ruiz, *Fontes Iuris Romani*, iii (Florence, 1943), 438.
[2] *BG* vi. 22. 4.

however scanty it might be, was hardly less than that of the most influential leaders.[1] This penetrating analysis, which he says was derived from some of the clansmen themselves, forms the converse of a fact which was later to be remarked by Tacitus: as wealth accumulates in a primitive society, power—and he means coercive power—tends to become concentrated in one central authority.[2]

In peacetime there was no chieftain in Caesar's day whose influence extended over all the clans which made up a people (*civitas*). The leading men of the tribes (*pagi*) into which each people was divided would do what they could to patch up such disputes as arose and to reconcile the contending parties. But in doing so they seem to have been nothing more than mediators: they will have had no coercive power. Moreover, Caesar's words suggest that the leading men of each tribe or 'region' acted only in those disputes which broke out between members of their own respective tribe or region: they are not said to have acted in disputes which broke out between persons belonging to different tribes or different regions.[3] For such disputes there was no mediatory body at this date, so far as we know. Further, as we have seen, the arable was allocated every year to the clans by the leading men. Who were these leading men? Did the leading men of the people as a whole meet together specifically for this purpose, or was the alloca-

---

[1] Ibid., vi. 22. 3 f. 'ne latos finis parare studeant, potentioresque humiliores possessionibus expellant, . . . ne qua oriatur pecuniae cupiditas, qua ex re factiones dissensionesque nascuntur; ut animi aequitate plebem contineant, cum suas quisque opes cum potentissimis aequari videat'.

[2] Tacitus, *G* xliv. 2 'est apud illos et opibus honos, eoque unus imperitat, nullis iam exceptionibus, non precario iure parendi'. Whether this was in fact true of the first-century Swedes is of course another question.

[3] Caesar, *BG* vi. 23. 5 *inter suos*.

tion discussed and carried out independently by the leading men of each tribe or group of clans? Was the allocation a centralized operation performed by one supreme body with the right to act in all parts of the people's territory, or did it consist of a number of purely local actions? The answer can scarcely be in doubt. It is hardly credible that any clan or group of clans would have consented to have their arable distributed among them by men who might come from a wholly different part of the country and who might know little or nothing about local conditions, the relative size of the various clans, the quality of the soil, and so on. The site of the arable and the allocation of it to the clans must have been decided upon by the leading men of each tribe or group of adjacent clans and not by a central council of the leading men of the whole people.[1] From this it might be inferred that in addition to the general assembly of the warriors of the whole people (see below) there was also a tribal assembly in each *pagus*, for the leading men presumably announced their decision on the arable to a meeting of all the persons concerned.

The various clans, then, were not bound together to any detectable extent under one central organ of government in time of peace. Evidently the clans or groups of clans lived more or less independently in their internal affairs, and on at least some occasions they could act independently even in their external relations. Late in the second century A.D. certain Germanic peoples of central Europe, who were in process of surrendering to the Emperor Marcus Aurelius, negotiated with him clan by clan, though others did so people by people;[2] and in

[1] I take *universis* in Tacitus, *G* xxvi. 1, to mean all the members of the one *pagus*.

[2] Dio Cassius, lxxi. 11. 3 οἱ μὲν κατὰ γένη οἱ δὲ καὶ κατὰ ἔθνη ἐπρεσβεύσαντο.

the interval since Caesar's time there is not likely to have been an increase in the kindreds' power to conduct external affairs—we shall see that the whole tendency in this period was towards more centralization. There is no reason to doubt that the clans lived on the basis of more or less complete equality. And similarly within the framework of the clan the individual's freedom from coercion and from imposed authority forced itself upon the notice of more than one Roman observer.[1]

A central council of the leading men did come into existence, however, in times of danger; and Caesar shows that in a moment of emergency it could take military decisions and lay down strategical plans. For when the Romans unexpectedly bridged the Rhine in 55 B.C. the leading men of the Suebi 'according to their custom' held a council and sent messengers in all directions ordering the womenfolk, the children, and the movable property to be taken from the settlements to the forests, and directing all able-bodied warriors to assemble.[2] What does Caesar mean when he says that this council met 'according to their custom' (*more suo*)? Does he refer to their custom in time of emergency, or does he imply that regular meetings of the council were held even in peacetime and that the Roman invasion

---

[1] Caesar, *BG* iv. 1. 9; Tacitus, *G* xi. 3, *H* iv. 76, *A* xiii. 54. 5 f.; Dio Cassius, lvi. 18. 2.

[2] Caesar, *BG* iv. 19. 2 *concilio*. That the reference is to a council of the leading men and not to a general assembly of the warriors is shown by the fact that 'omnes qui arma ferre possent' were not present. But *concilio*, ibid., vi. 23. 7, is the assembly of the warriors: the word is so used in Tacitus, *G* xii. 1, xiii. 1. But it might be argued that Caesar's usage is in fact consistent and that *concilio* in *BG* vi. 23. 7 is also the council of the leading men. On this view the evidence for the assembly of the warriors in Caesar's time would vanish. It would follow (*a*) that the *comitatus* in the mid first century B.C. was confined to the *principes* (which in any case may well be more or less true), and (*b*) that the general assembly of all the warriors came into existence between the time of Caesar and that of Tacitus.

coincided with one of these regular meetings? If the latter, this is our only explicit evidence for a central council of the leading men of the whole people in peacetime. But if, as we have seen reason to believe, the administration of justice and the allocation of the arable lay outside the scope of any such council, what then were its functions? It is hard to give a wholly satisfactory answer, and hence it is not clear that in time of peace there was any council of elders or leading men which would meet and exert influence over the people as a whole, though such a council certainly met when danger threatened. In peacetime no council higher than the councils of the *pagi* can be said with certainty to have existed.

In time of war an unknown number of confederate chieftains was elected, and Caesar gives no hint that any one of them had greater authority or prestige than the others: they were joint leaders. As long as the war lasted, they are said, whether rightly or wrongly, to have had the power of life and death over the warriors whom they led.[1] It was still the case among some Germanic peoples of Tacitus' day (p. 32 below) and among the Visigoths in the time of Ulfila that there was normally no one over-all peacetime chieftain. Among some at least of the Franks in the early fourth century the same was true: they, too, elected their chiefs only on the eve of war.[2] The case of the Saxons shows that the type of chieftainship which Caesar describes had not wholly disappeared even in the eighth century A.D. At that date the Saxon war-leader was chosen only on

[1] Caesar, *BG* vi. 23. 4. But perhaps they had this power only in cases of desertion, treachery, cowardice, and the like.
[2] *Paneg. Lat.* xii (ix). 22. 3 'lectis eruptionis auctoribus'. For the Alamanni see p. 40 below, and for the Visigoths *Nottingham Medieval Studies* v (1961), 20 f.

the outbreak of war (though he was chosen, curiously enough, not by election but by lot from among the tribal leaders); and when the war was over he reverted, as his predecessors of Caesar's time appear to have done, to the position of an ordinary tribal leader. The difference between this and what Caesar describes (apart from the use of lot) is that among the Saxons there was only one war-leader, whereas there were several among Caesar's Germans.[1] Nor was the multiple war-leadership quick to disappear in all parts of Germany. It could still be found among the Franks early in the fourth century, among the Burgundians towards its close, and among the Alamanni until the year 536.[2] Even in Caesar's time, however, the tendency may have been growing to limit to two the number of confederate war-chiefs; for in 58 B.C. Caesar heard that a force of Suebi had come down to the Rhine under the leadership of two brothers named Nasua and Cimberius, and in later ages this dual command was exceedingly widespread among the Germanic peoples (p. 39 n. 1 below). But only this one example of it has been recorded from the first century B.C.[3] Unfortunately, we catch only a few glimpses of the war-chieftains in Caesar's time. Ariovistus insisted on being accompanied by ten men when

[1] Bede, *HE* v. 10; cf. *Vita Lebuini Antiqua* iv (*MGH, Scriptores*, xxx, 2, 793); Poeta Saxo, i. 23 f. (*MGH, Poetae Lat. Aevi Carolini*, iv, 8), writing in the ninth century, 'plebs omnis habebat quot pagos tot pene duces', and the whole passage. I refer more than once to the Saxons because of their exceptionally primitive social life even in the eighth century.

[2] *Paneg. Lat.*, loc. cit.; Amm. Marc. xxviii. 5. 10; W. Veeck, *Die Alamannen in Württemberg* (Berlin and Leipzig, 1931), i, 108 ff. The Frankish force which invaded Gaul in 388 was led by three chieftains: Greg. Tur., *HF* ii. 9 *init.*

[3] Caesar, *BG* i. 37. 3. Greg. Tur., *HF* ii. 9, found a reference in one of his authorities to two *regales* of the Franks, and remarks: 'cum autem eos regales vocet, nescimus utrum reges fuerint an in vices tenuerunt regnum'. Why does he make this last suggestion? There seems to be no evidence for an alternating leadership among the early Germans.

he negotiated with Caesar, who unhappily gives no information about the status of these ten. An important decision concerning the Ubii was expected to be made at a time of danger by their 'leading men and their senate', as Caesar puts it; and the two terms are not synonymous. And in wartime the Usipetes and Tencteri came to negotiate with Caesar 'with all their leading men and elders'; and again Caesar refers to their chieftains and their council.[1] In none of these cases did the chieftains act without the council. There is no certain evidence for individual, personal authority in early Germany.

Besides the council and the war-chieftainship there was also a general assembly of the warriors.[2] But Caesar gives no description of its powers, and we shall return to it when we come to discuss the evidence given by Tacitus.

In the middle of the first century B.C., then, a Germanic people was composed of a number of kindreds or clans which were the basic economic units of society, though the acquisition of herds of cattle by individual warriors may have been tending to introduce differences of wealth into the clans and so to detach the individual from his kindred. These clans were grouped together in larger units which we have called 'tribes' (*pagi*). Of these little is known, but it seems that the leading men of each tribe formed a council which allocated the arable land every year and that they acted as mediators in disputes which broke out within the tribe. There is no clear evidence, however, for the existence of a central, confederate council of the elders or leading men of the whole people, except in wartime. In wartime

[1] Caesar, *BG* i. 43. 3, iv. 11. 3, 13. 4.
[2] Ibid., vi. 23. 7, though see p. 12 n. 2 above.

a number of elected chieftains led the forces of the people, for the various tribes federated at least to this extent that they put their military forces under some sort of central leadership. But there is no trace of any institutions of coercion, except perhaps in war; and the evidence seems to point to the conclusion that in peace-time there was nothing which could be called a central-ized public power over and above the armed warriors themselves. As for slaves, ancient authors give little information about the nature of Germanic slavery in the period before the Migrations.[1] Their hints suggest that domestic slavery was restricted to females, that the chief function of the slave trade in Germany was to convey slaves from the interior of the country to the Roman frontier for sale to the Romans, that several Germanic peoples killed off their prisoners or at any rate their adult male prisoners after a successful campaign, that it was difficult to hold an adult male German in slavery in Germany, and hence that most of such slaves as existed there were put to work on the land in very favourable conditions: they were given a 'home' (*penates*) of their own and were merely required to pay their owner a quantity of grain, cattle, or cloth. In view of all this and of the constant demand for slaves on the Roman frontier and the ease and profit with which they could be dis-posed of there, it seems fair to conclude that the number of slaves in early Germany was small (except in one or two places which were exposed to abnormally strong Roman influence) and that such slaves as did exist there were to a large extent of non-Germanic birth. In view of this and of the absence of grounds for serious tension

[1] The evidence relating to slavery in early Germany is collected and discussed *apud* M. I. Finley (editor), *Slavery in Classical Antiquity* (Heffer, Cambridge, 1960), 191–203.

among the free population, organs of repression were not required and did not exist.

### 3. From Caesar to Tacitus

In Caesar's time, then, Germanic society was more primitive than is sometimes supposed. The fact that the arable was still worked communally by the kindreds and that any given piece of arable was cultivated for only one year suggests that the techniques of agriculture were still at a low stage of development. The kindred and not the monogamous family was still the fundamental entity in society. In the kindreds of Caesar's time descent may still have been reckoned in the female line for many purposes, perhaps for most.[1] The kindreds were only loosely knit together, and in peacetime there seems to have been no public authority to weld them all into a unity. Slavery was still in an incipient stage of growth, and there were no public institutions of coercion. In all, so primitive was Germanic society that we cannot disregard Caesar's remark that the life of the Germans was one of poverty, want, and hardship.[2]

[1] On matrilineal descent among the Germans see in English H. M. Chadwick, *The Origin of the English Nation* (Cambridge, 1907), 306 ff.; Bertha Phillpotts, *Kindred and Clan in the Middle Ages and After* (Cambridge, 1913), 265 ff.; R. Briffault, *The Mothers* (London, 1927), i, 414–17; V. Grönbech, *The Culture of the Teutons* (London and Copenhagen, 1931), i, 347 ff. The transition to father-right was still historically recent among the Germans of whom Tacitus speaks and was still incomplete. Before Roman civilization reached the borders of Germany and brought about the rapid social changes which will be discussed later, the matrilineal principle may have been in full force among some at least of the peoples even of western Germany (to say nothing of those of the remote north and east) and perhaps among a majority of them.

[2] *BG* vi. 24. 4. On the other hand, they may have been able to withdraw numbers of men for a considerable time from the business of food-production. If the embankment mentioned by Tacitus, *A* ii. 19. 3, has been correctly identified at Leese on the Weser it was a structure 1,800 metres long, 2½ metres high, and 10 metres broad: G. Bersu and others, *Prähistorische Zeitschrift*, xvii (1926), 100–31. But this may have been built by the forced labour of war-prisoners.

Now in the time of Tacitus a number of changes had come over Germanic society, which will be discussed later. But there is one change that must be mentioned here. At the end of the first century A.D. the kindred was less decisively the basis of society than it had been in Caesar's day, and one indication of this decline in its importance concerns the distribution of the arable. True, a decision had still to be reached every year as to which tract or tracts of the people's land in each *pagus* or in each village was to be brought under the plough. But when this was done, the land was no longer divided up among the clans to be worked in common by the clansmen,[1] and so its crops cannot any longer have been appropriated in common by the kindreds. The procedure described by Caesar had been modified; for Tacitus reports that the arable was now distributed 'according to social standing', a phrase which shows that it was distributed not to kindreds but to individuals, the leading men of the *pagus* each taking a larger or a more fertile allotment than a rank-and-file warrior, and the wealthier or more renowned of the warriors presumably taking more than the less wealthy or the less renowned.[2] The kindred was no longer of basic importance where the arable and its produce were concerned. How had this change come about? And what was its significance?

It may be assumed that such potters as used the wheel—and these were very few—together with many of the smiths and, where they existed, the miners and iron-smelters[3] were full-time specialists at their work,

[1] Tacitus, *G* xv. 1 *ex familia*.

[2] Ibid., xxvi. 1 *secundum dignationem*. But for a case of clan-ownership of land many centuries after Tacitus' day see *Lex Alamann.* lxxxiv.

[3] For these see e.g. A. Stieren, *Germania*, xix (1935), 12–20; H. Hingst, *Offa*, xi (1952), 28–37; H. Hinz, ibid., 37–42; etc.

and did not directly produce their own food-supply. They produced commodities—that is, articles produced for sale or exchange and not for consumption by the producers—and these commodities they exchanged for food produced by others. The Germans had also discovered that men might be treated as commodities: they, too, might be bought and sold. To what extent the production of commodities and the trade which resulted from it had developed beyond this point in the first century B.C. is a matter of equal importance and obscurity. Leaving aside sporadic cases where the plunder or prisoners taken in a successful raid were profitably sold or where a crop failed locally or where the cattle belonging to a community became diseased or were lost in an enemy raid—leaving aside these and similar local or temporary occasions of plenty or of scarcity, the Germanic village is unlikely to have used many objects which had not been produced at home, though a limited number of private individuals certainly bought metals, including silver.[1] In fact, the private ownership of the herds and of articles of luxury is proof of private trading between individuals. But many communities as such were obliged to buy articles, like iron and salt, which were not produced everywhere. Indeed, it may be that when the Hermunduri and the Chatti fought a war in A.D. 58 for the possession of a salt-bed they aimed not merely at covering their own needs but also at exporting salt at a profit to those peoples who were in need of it.[2] In the main, then, two kinds of article were bartered in Germany in Caesar's time: (a) essential articles which

[1] Caesar, *BG* vi. 28. 6.
[2] Tacitus, *A* xiii. 57 f., who stresses the religious aspect of the struggle, cf. Uslar, op. cit. 169. For other German salt-wars see Amm. Marc. xxviii. 5. 11; *Annales Fuldenses*, s.a. 892. The export of salt from the Empire to the barbarians is prohibited in *Digest*, xxxix. 4. 11.

were required by a community as a whole, and (b) luxury articles which were owned by individuals. It is not difficult to guess which of these two kinds of trade was gaining ground proportionately to the other in the years which followed Caesar's arrival on the Rhine. Soon after Caesar's time exchange between individuals—for example, cattle or men in exchange for metals or for furs—was undoubtedly gaining ground relatively to trade conducted for the benefit of a community. For while the demand of many peoples for articles which could not be made at home may or may not have increased in the period between Caesar and Tacitus, the archaeological evidence shows that the leading men's demand for luxuries increased drastically.

Celtic merchants dealing in Italian as well as Celtic wares were active in Germany in the middle of the first century B.C. and reached some areas in considerable numbers. They supplied the more well-to-do warriors with foreign articles like wine, various kinds of bronze vessels, and so on.[1] But the goods imported by the Germans from the Celtic merchants were much less in quantity and variety than the goods which they bought from Roman merchants in the early years of the Christian era. For with the Roman occupation of western Germany in 12–9 B.C. the German leaders were able to buy whole categories of luxury goods—glass vessels, red table ware, Roman weapons, brooches, statuettes, ornaments of various kinds, and so on—which had not

---

[1] Caesar, *BG* i. 39. 1, iv. 2. 1 and 6, 3. 3; H. J. Eggers, *Der römische Import im freien Germanien* (Hamburg, 1951), 40, 42. For wine, etc., see Poseidonius, 87 F 22 (Jacoby); Caesar, *BG* ii. 15. 4, iv. 2. 6, where the ban of the Nervii and Suebi on the import of wine and 'reliquae res ad luxuriam pertinentes' (what are these?) suggests that other Germanic peoples permitted such imports.

reached them before.[1] And the fact that Roman goods could now be bought stimulated the desire of the leading men of the Germans to have them. These imported luxuries were highly prized and seem to have had an enormous prestige-value. They were privately owned, and from the beginning of the Christian era they existed in great numbers.

From at least the time of Augustus many a Roman trader penetrated deep into Germany hawking his goods from settlement to settlement.[2] There is reason to think, however, that the majority of Roman traders carried on their business with the lands lying immediately outside the Imperial frontier and that many of the Roman goods which reached the interior of Germany did so by being passed from hand to hand among the Germans themselves.[3] If so, they thereby stimulated throughout the whole of Germany and not merely along the frontier the production, or at any rate the acquisition, by the Germans themselves of commodities which could be used to pay for the imported luxuries. The dimensions of this trade must be emphasized. There was even a permanent settlement of Romans residing and earning their living by trade and moneylending in a

[1] Eggers, op. cit. 38, 42 f. Contrast his Karte 3 with his Karte 4. But the extent of the wine-trade in early Germany should not be exaggerated: see R. Nierhaus, *Acta Archaeologica*, xxv (1954), 254 f.

[2] Eggers, op. cit. 36 f., 67 ff.; R. E. M. Wheeler, *Rome Beyond the Imperial Frontiers* (London, 1954), 11 ff. For some of the dangers which beset traders who ventured in among the barbarian peoples see Dio Cassius, liii. 26. 4, with R. Syme, *Cambridge Ancient History*, x, 348. (Did the barbarians of the Valais kill these traders because they were traders or because they were Romans?) Note the attack on Roman *negotiatores* in Tacitus, *H* iv. 15; and for a vivid picture of a traveller of a later date in the sparsely inhabited forests of Germany see Eigil, *Vita S. Sturmi* vii–ix (*MGH, Scriptores*, ii, 368 f.), which *mutatis mutandis* gives some impression of the solitude and perils of earlier travellers.

[3] S. Bolin, *XIX Bericht d. röm.-germ. Kommission* (1929), 140; H. Aubin, 'Der Rheinhandel in römischer Zeit', *Bonner Jahrbücher*, cxxx (1925), 30; cf. Wheeler, op. cit. 177 f.

Germanic chieftain's capital in and about A.D. 19. This was the capital of the Marcomanni in Bohemia, and the goods which these traders imported came in particular from the Danubian provinces, especially Noricum, but also in part from Italy and Gaul. For a time Bohemia imported Roman goods on a scale unparalleled among the Germanic peoples. It is true that soon after A.D. 19 this Marcomannic trade declined and lost its exceptional character—no doubt for one reason or another the community of Roman merchants had been dispersed. But permanent settlements of Roman traders beyond any Roman frontier are very rarely mentioned in Imperial times by our authorities, and no doubt were in fact very unusual; and that traders should have found it worth their while to settle among the Marcomanni illustrates the size of the demand for Roman goods in Bohemia.[1] That the Imperial government itself recognized the importance of this trade would be proved strikingly if it is true that it had secured in a formal treaty with the Marcomanni the right for these traders to carry on their work in Bohemia.[2] But although Bohemia was exceptional in the degree of its demand for imported luxuries, it was exceptional in degree only: the demand for Roman commodities was exceedingly widespread among the more well-to-do tribesmen throughout the length and breadth of continental Germany.

The importance of money in this process must not be exaggerated. The general practice even at the end of the first century A.D., especially in the interior of Germany, was exchange by barter.[3] But in regions near the

[1] Tacitus, *A* ii. 62. 4; cf. *H* iv. 15; Eggers, op. cit. 47, 51; O. Almgren, *Mannus*, v (1913), 265–78.

[2] See e.g. Furneaux on Tacitus, *A* loc. cit., and most recently Wheeler, op. cit. 20.

[3] Tacitus, *G* v. 4 f. Note the use of cattle ibid., xii. 2, xviii. 2, xxi. 1.

frontier where trade with Roman merchants was particularly brisk commodities were often paid for in
Roman coins in the first century A.D.[1] On the other
hand, the vast numbers of Roman coins which have been
found in the interior of Germany and which were
privately owned by individual Germans were regarded
as ornaments rather than as a medium of exchange.[2]
Hence, if the general effect of the introduction of
Roman money was to hasten the disintegration of the
clans, the extent to which it did so must not be over-
stated. Tacitus notes explicitly that the lending of money
on interest was unknown among the Germanic peoples,[3]
and the appearance of the Germanic moneylender still
lay in the future—though perhaps not in the very distant future, for by the time of Tacitus, both in Bohemia
and in the lower Rhine area,[4] the Romans had introduced the practice of lending money on interest.

Between the time of Caesar, then, and that of Tacitus
(a) there was a striking increase in the number and
value of the goods imported into Germany from abroad,
(b) this phenomenon, though more intense in some
areas than in others, was universal throughout Germany, and (c) the goods imported were to a large extent
owned by individuals and not collectively by the
kindreds, for it will scarcely be thought that glass,
bronze, textiles, pottery, wine, weapons, coins, and so
on, were owned communally.[5] But how did the individual German warriors pay for the commodities which

[1] Ibid., v. 4 f.
[2] Wheeler, op. cit. 63–6, seems more judicious than Bolin, art. cit.
143 f. In Scandinavia at the turn of the second and third centuries coins
were not used as a means of payment in daily trade: H. Shetelig and
H. Falk, *Scandinavian Archaeology* (Oxford, 1937), 201.
[3] *G* xxvi. 1.
[4] Id., *H* iv. 15 *negotiatores*.
[5] Cf. Clara Redlich, *Forschungen und Fortschritte*, xxiv (1948), 177–80.

they now imported on a more lavish scale than formerly? Some of them earned Roman money by serving in the Roman army, and some received payments from the Imperial government for good behaviour (p. 97 below); but coins, as we have seen, were themselves usually regarded as commodities, and these sources of income will not account for the extraordinary increase in the number of Roman objects which reached all parts of Germany in the early Imperial period. The problem is not simplified by the fact that the general technical level and the division of labour in Germany were such that there could be no large-scale export of manufactured goods to an Empire which had at its disposal far larger quantities of such goods than had any of its neighbours. Amber, of course, was a local product of the Baltic shores, though in so far as it reached the Roman frontier as the result of being traded from one Germanic people to another it will have stimulated the acquisition of commodities among other peoples than those who originally gathered it. But it cannot account for a phenomenon which was universal throughout Germany. On the whole, then, it may be assumed that two commodities above all others were used to pay for Roman goods—cattle and slaves, both of which were privately owned in Caesar's time. The problem is, however: how did the individual warriors obtain enough privately-owned commodities to pay for a quantity of imports *which was vastly greater* than that which they had paid for in Caesar's time? How did they *increase* to such an extent the number of commodities available to them for barter?

It is tempting to think that the increased demand for slaves and cattle must have increased the frequency of wars, of cattle-raids, and of slave-raids beyond anything that had been known before the middle of the first century B.C. As for slave raids, consider the case of the West African coast when slave-dealing Europeans first arrived there. Slavery had been known in West Africa before that time, but it was normally of a mild and patriarchal character, perhaps not much more severe than that which Tacitus describes among the Germans. But the arrival of Europeans with attractive goods to offer in exchange for slaves brought about a disastrous increase in the frequency of slave-raiding among the Africans of the coast. Indeed, it altered the whole nature of native warfare and brought it about that 'the coast tribes were nothing more than slave catchers and kidnappers' who left entire regions of the interior depopulated after their raids. It introduced a brutal conception of slavery which had hitherto been unknown among the Africans.[1] The arrival of the Romans on the Rhine and the Danube may not have brought about such calamitous conditions; but is it possible to believe that it caused no change at all?

In any event, their intensified concentration on acquiring goods which could be disposed of privately without the interference of the kindreds turned the eyes of the leading men towards the produce of the arable land. That they exerted themselves to convert the produce of the arable into private property, and that they did so not without success, is proved by the new system of allocating the arable which had come into existence before the end of the first century A.D. The soil was now tilled by individual cultivators each working on his own account, and no more is heard of the collective working of the clan holding. Although private ownership of land

[1] G. Landtman, *The Origin of the Inequality of the Social Classes* (London, 1938), 268, with references.

was still unknown—it could not develop fully when the one piece of land was cultivated by the one person for a year only—the time of its appearance had now come perceptibly closer than it was in Caesar's day. With further advances in agricultural techniques—with an extension, for example, of the marling which was already practised by the Ubii in the middle of the first century A.D. and which fertilized their fields for as much as ten years (p. 4 above)—fewer fallow periods would be necessary and the re-siting and re-allocating of the arable would become less frequent. Private ownership and inheritance of land would then be possible. But that stage had not been generally reached at the time when Tacitus was writing.[1]

But if his flocks and herds were the main source of a German leader's wealth, would the right to dispose freely of a share of his clan's crops have materially improved his position? It is not certain that the Germans of the late first century A.D. were pastoralists to an equal degree with their ancestors of Caesar's day. True, they still measured wealth in terms of cattle,[2] but it is difficult to resist the impression that the general level of the Germans' agricultural techniques must have been raised substantially as a result of the normal improvement which might be expected in the course of 150 years among a people at this stage of development, especially in view of their contact with the Romans. When the Romans occupied the Rhineland a more intensive agriculture at once made its appearance there far surpassing the pre-Roman, and the crafts and in-

---

[1] In some parts of Germany private ownership of land may already have been known, Tacitus, *H* v. 23 'agros villasque Civilis', but the Batavians were in some sense incorporated in the Empire; and id., *G* xxvi. 1 shows this to have been exceptional.

[2] Ibid., v. 2.

dustries in the larger settlements reached a height which had hitherto been undreamed of.[1] Archaeology has shown that even in distant Scandinavia 'all the ordinary daily tools, large or small, were made in imitation of Roman technique, which in this sphere was the standard', while the influence of Roman taste extends 'in general to all the Germanic forms of ornaments, implements, earthenware vessels, belonging to the [first] two centuries'.[2] Moreover, entirely new tools and skills, from the scissors and the distaff to the art of sailing, were introduced about this time into Germany; and it can scarcely be doubted that as a result of technical improvements the value of the arable land was increased appreciably. And Caesar himself admits that even in his day, if a Germanic people were prevented by the raids of a more powerful neighbour from sowing and reaping their crops for a sufficient time, they would have to move away from their homes altogether to some place of greater safety.[3] The value to individual Germans of the produce of the arable, therefore, may not have been negligible.

There are two fixed points in the historical process under discussion: (a) the communal sharing and working of the arable by the kindreds in Caesar's time, which is attested explicitly and indeed emphatically by Caesar himself (p. 8 n. 2 above), and (b) the individual working of the arable in the days of Tacitus, which is an inescapable inference from Tacitus' words. Our problem is: why was the earlier system transformed into the later?

---

[1] So K. Schumacher, *Siedlungs- und Kulturgeschichte der Rheinlande* (Mainz, 1923), ii, 246. Roman ploughs were exported to Germany: ibid., 249.

[2] Shetelig and Falk, op. cit. 198 ff.; G. Ekholm, *Cambridge Ancient History*, xi, 73.

[3] Caesar, *BG* iv. 1. 2; cf. 4. 1; Dio Cassius, lxxi. 20. 1.

There was a tendency even in Caesar's day or soon after it for 'private' trading to increase relatively to communal trading. The leading men owned cattle privately and so were in a position to add to their well-being, their prestige, and their social standing by buying the silver, the bronze vessels, the wine, and so forth, which traders displayed before them. But this tendency was sharply accelerated by the arrival of Roman civilization on the Rhine and the Danube and for a moment even on the Elbe, for there was now a greater array of goods for the leading men to acquire. The notables in all parts of Germany now distinguished themselves from the rank and file of the warriors and even from their own kinsmen by possessing themselves of imported Roman luxuries on a scale previously unknown. Hence, by the time of Tacitus differences of wealth inside the kindred itself were so substantial that the framework of the clan was undermined, the old communal working of the land disappeared, and the time was nearer at hand when the arable would be freely owned by private persons in Germany.

It would no doubt be possible to overemphasize the part played by the Romans in this process, and a similar result would unquestionably have been reached, though perhaps more slowly, even if the Romans had never appeared on the scene. With gradual improvement of agricultural techniques and the resulting increase in the value of the produce of the arable land the leading men among the Germans would no doubt have found ways and means of ridding themselves of the traditional ways even in the absence of the Romans.

# CHAPTER TWO

# THE GERMANS IN THE TIME OF TACITUS

TACITUS discusses a number of aspects of Germanic society which Caesar scarcely mentions at all. The earlier history of several institutions described by Tacitus, therefore, is obscure. Consequently, when we try to trace the developments which took place between the times of our two great authorities we had best confine ourselves so far as possible to those institutions which are described by them both.

## *1. The Council, the Chieftainship, and the Assembly*

The council of the leading men existed among the Germans in Caesar's day, at any rate in wartime; but in the period to which Tacitus refers it existed in peace-time as well as in war. Who were these leading men (*principes*)? In Tacitus' day the sons of all Germanic warriors were taken at the age of puberty into the general assembly of the warriors and were there presented with a shield and spear to denote that they themselves were now warriors. But the status of a *princeps* was given only to those of them who could claim noble birth or who could point to outstanding services on the part of their fathers. These then went on to serve in one of the 'retinues', which will be discussed later. Having won glory in a retinue such a warrior would take his place at the deliberations of the leading men; but, although Arminius was elected chief of the Cherusci at the age of 26, a young warrior would not normally wield as much influence as his seniors.[1] This is the only way of becoming a *princeps* which Tacitus records, and no doubt it was the only way of becoming one. But what does 'noble birth' mean in this connexion? Doubtless Tacitus means that the young man in question was usually descended from a line of comparatively rich and distinguished ancestors. But we happen to know that the phrase might also denote simply that his father had performed outstanding military services regardless of his wealth.[2] Hence, at first sight it might appear that the council was not altogether a closed circle of those whose fathers had won considerable wealth in the past. But this is not wholly the case. Even in the winning of military glory the poor man was at a disadvantage to the more well-to-do warrior, for a poor man's arms and armour would be markedly inferior to those of his richer neighbour: he would probably have no sword, and he would certainly have no helmet or breastplate (p. 113 below). Hence, the wealthy were in a better position than the poor to perform outstanding military services for the community; and it looks as though the 'leading men' were normally the wealthy men. Whether a man of undistinguished parentage could become a *princeps* at all in the time of which Tacitus is speaking is not clearly stated; but it is never said of any Germanic *princeps* that he was not of noble birth.

[1] Tacitus, *G* xiii. 1–2; cf. xi. 5 *aetas*, which refers, however, to meetings of the assembly. For a later period cf. Claudian, *BG* 479 ff., and note also Homer, *Il.* xiv. 110 ff.

[2] Tacitus, *H* iv. 15 'erat in Canninefatibus stolidae audaciae Brinno, claritate natalium insigni: pater eius multa hostilia ausus Gaianarum expeditionum ludibrium impune spreverat', suggests that *insignis nobilitas* (*G* xiii. 2) could be identical with *magna patrum merita*. The importance of noble birth may have been read into Germanic society by Tacitus, as modern scholars have read it into Homeric society: G. M. Calhoun, *Classical Philology*, xxix (1934), 192–208, 301–16. There is no evidence that in Tacitus' time the chiefs' power rested on any claims to a divine origin or descent.

Unfortunately, there is no information about the relation of the leading men to the tribes (*pagi*). Was each tribe necessarily represented on the council of the leading men? If so, what was the usual number of representatives? Did the *pagi* have equal representation on the council? How large was the council? We do not know. But other problems are less obscure. The council, according to Tacitus, dealt with matters of minor importance affecting the people as a whole, while the most weighty business was decided by the assembly of the warriors. (No doubt, however, the council had executive power in moments of emergency, as it had had in Caesar's time.) But even affairs which came to the assembly were discussed beforehand by the council.[1] Whether a matter was sufficiently important to come before the assembly was a point which was presumably decided by custom and usage: the warriors in general would know what *sort* of thing might be decided by the council and what *sort* of business had always been laid before the assembly. At any rate, although the people were sovereign, the influence of these leading men was considerable, and without them it was difficult for the warriors at large to initiate any venture of consequence.[2]

[1] Tacitus, *G* xi. 1. The earliest extant description of a Germanic council meeting is in the *Vita Lebuini Antiqua* vi (p. 14 n. 1 above): 'tunc in unum conglobati fecerunt iuxta ritum in primis supplicationem ad deos, postulantes tuitionem deorum patriae suae et ut possent in ipso conventu statuere sibi utilia et quae forent placita omnibus diis. deinde disposito grandi orbe contionari coeperunt'. But this Saxon council was different in its composition from those of which Tacitus speaks: see p. 42 n. 1 below. For a nice example of the preliminary discussion of an important question by a Swedish *rex* and his *principes* in A.D. 852 see Rimbertus, *Vita S. Anskarii* xxvii (pp. 57 f., ed. Waitz).

[2] Tacitus, *A* i. 55. 3; cf. *Paneg. Lat.* vi (vii). 11. 6 'cladem suam, quamvis multi pereant, vulgus ignorat; compendium est devincendorum hostium duces sustulisse'. For a later time see *Heimskringla: Harald the Stern*, xliv. Could the assembly even meet if the *rex* for some reason were absent? Note Rimbertus, op. cit. xix (p. 41 f.) on the Swedes of Birca when

In some sense, then, the leading men were becoming the decisive element in Germanic society in the first century A.D., though this is a matter to which we shall have to return (p. 47 f. below).

The second great organ of society was the military chieftainship. In Caesar's day there had been no peace-time chiefs, and the war-chiefs held their position for the duration of a specific war and no longer. But Tacitus speaks of two kinds of chieftainship which could be found among the various Germanic peoples of his day. One type was elective, and any warrior might be chosen provided that his valour and capacity were sufficiently outstanding.[1] He is called the *dux*. His duties appear to have been wholly military, and the people were represented at religious ceremonies not by him but by a person whom Tacitus calls *princeps civitatis* and who probably had no other important function than the religious one which Tacitus assigns to him here.[2] It is not clear for how long a chief of this kind held his office. Since the primitive Germanic communities are not known to have limited an elective office to a specified number of years, it looks as though his position was identical with that of the war-chiefs of whom Caesar speaks—he held office only for the duration of the war which he had been elected to fight. A case is known from the first century A.D. which seems to support this conclusion. The first move of the Canninefates in A.D. 69,

they were actually threatened by a Danish attack: 'et forte tunc rex ipsorum longius inde aberat, et principes ac populi multitudo congregari non poterant'; but this, of course, like Homer, *Od.* ii. 26 f., is not conclusive for Tacitus' time.

[1] *G* vii. 1 'reges ex nobilitate duces ex virtute sumunt'. It should not be supposed that both a *rex* and a *dux* could be found among any one people: they are alternative and exclusive types of chief.

[2] Ibid. x. 4, with Anderson ad loc., though Arminius should not be described as a *princeps civitatis*. See H. M. Chadwick, 'The Ancient Teutonic Priesthood', *Folk-Lore*, xi (1900), 276 n. 4.

when they decided to join in Civilis' revolt against the Romans, was to elect a certain Brinno as their leader (p. 30 n. 2 above); and the implication would seem to be either that they had no chief at all in time of peace or that the peacetime chief was not identical with their leader in war. But since it is scarcely possible in the total absence of evidence to assume the existence of a peacetime leader who was not also war-chief, it seems safest to suppose that the conditions depicted by Caesar could still be found in the age of Tacitus, that among some Germanic peoples there was no confederate leader in peacetime, and that the war-leader was still elected only for the duration of a given war. This seems all the more probable since examples are known which date from far later periods (p. 13 above). But there is one essential difference between this type of leadership as Tacitus describes it and as it had been observed by Caesar: a number of war-leaders were elected in the first century B.C., all apparently with equal powers, whereas now only one such chief or at most two (p. 39 below) were elected for any one war. In wartime, power (such as it is) has been concentrated into one man's hands, and the fact would not have surprised Tacitus, whose view on the concentration of power has already been mentioned (p. 10 n. 2 above).

The second type of chieftainship mentioned by Tacitus differed from the first in two respects and was clearly a later, more developed, and less egalitarian form of the institution; and there is no parallel to it in Caesar. This type of chief, whom Tacitus in his *Germania*[1] calls a 'king' (*rex*), was also elective. But what

---

[1] vii. 1, quoted on p. 32, n. 1 above. But we must not expect Tacitus to use the words *rex* and *dux* in this precise technical sense throughout the whole corpus of his works.

does Tacitus mean when he says that the Germans chose chieftains of this type 'in accordance with their noble birth' (*ex nobilitate*)? There can be little doubt—for we must otherwise assume the existence of *three* distinct types of chief in the first century A.D.—that he is referring to a kind of chieftainship which he indicates elsewhere and which although elective was confined to the members of a recognized 'royal clan' or 'royal stock' (*stirps regia*) such as is known to have existed among the first-century Batavians and Cherusci, the sixth-century Heruls, and others. Any member of this royal clan was eligible for the military chieftainship and even if not elected would enjoy greater influence than a member of any other clan could hope to have.[1] It was not the case that only a chief's son could succeed to the leadership. Indeed, there is no conclusive evidence that any Germanic chieftain of the first century A.D. was followed as leader by his son (though cases are known where the leadership descended directly in the female line);[2] and

[1] Tacitus, *H* iv. 13, *A* xi. 16. 1, 3 *gentile decus*, 17. 2 (cf. ii. 10. 1 *imperator*); Procopius, *BG* vi. 14. 41, 15. 2 and 27 ff. (an extraordinary but credible story); cf. the 'nobile Marobodui et Tudri genus' of the Marcomanni and Quadi in Tacitus, *G* xlii. 2. Note also Adam of Bremen, iv. 22, on the eleventh-century Swedes: 'reges habent ex genere antiquo, quorum tamen vis pendet in populi sentencia; quod in commune omnes laudaverint, illum confirmare oportet, nisi eius decretum potius videatur, quod aliquando secuntur inviti'. (This quotation is continued on p. 37, n. 2 below.)

[2] The Cherusci are the only Germanic people of whom it can be said with certainty that their leadership descended in the male line before the time of Tacitus. True, it is not certain that Sigimer, the father of Arminius, had been war-chief: he may have been no more than a *princeps*. It is also true that we do not know who became military leader after Arminius' death. But Italicus, who was made their chief in A.D. 47, was Arminius' brother's son, a fact which proves that in the 'royal clan' descent was reckoned patrilineally. For if descent had been reckoned in the female line Italicus would have belonged to the kinship-group of his mother, who was the daughter of a chief of the Chatti and was not a Cheruscan at all. The abandonment of the matrilineal principle by the nobility or the 'royal clan' by no means implies its abandonment by the

34

it is far from probable that among any first-century people the chieftainship descended by hereditary right from father to son. The succession was open to any member of the royal clan and to no one except the members of that clan. If no other member of the royal clan were available the Cherusci at least were obliged to accept as their leader a member of it who had never seen Germany, who had never left the Imperial provinces, and whose father's career suggested that he would make anything but a loyal and popular leader. Among the Cherusci the restriction of the leadership to the royal clan was rigid and definitive, though no more so than among the Heruls half a millenium later.[1]

Again, a chief of this type unquestionably held office for life, and he had other duties besides military ones. He took part in certain religious rites. He might put proposals before the assembled warriors for their approval or rejection, though his proposals might be listened to with more or less respect according to his years, his noble birth, his fame as a warrior, or his eloquence.[2] In his deliberations with the council of the leading men it is unlikely that he would act contrary to their unanimous advice: indeed, he could be directly overruled by them (p. 37 below). No doubt the practice

community as a whole: see Miss Phillpotts, op. cit. (on p. 17 n. 1 above), 270 n. 1. Hence, the fact that the military chieftainship of the Cherusci descended in the male line does not prove that the patrilineal system was general throughout Cheruscan society in A.D. 47.

[1] Tacitus, *A* xi. 16 f.; Procopius, loc. cit. (with § 35); cf. id., *BG* viii. 25. 11.

[2] Tacitus, *G* x. 4, xi. 5, *A* i. 57. 1; Adam of Bremen, loc. cit.; Rimbertus, op. cit. xlvi (p. 57) on the ninth-century Swedes: 'sic quippe apud eos moris est ut quodcumque negotium publicum magis in populi unanimi voluntate quam in regia constet potestate'. When Ansgar asked permission to preach, the king knew that the mission might be unpopular: 'quapropter et ego hanc legationem vestram confirmare nec possum nec audeo, priusquam sortibus deos nostros consulam et populi quoque super hoc voluntatem interrogem'.

would vary according to the chief's prestige and strength of personality, but even the most secure chieftain would probably pay careful attention to custom and traditional usage.[1] He might well be treated with a considerable lack of formality by his followers. In the extreme case of the sixth-century Heruls the 'king' received no privileged treatment: any rank-and-file warrior was at liberty to sit with him and to eat with him and even to insult him at pleasure.[2] Among some post-Roman Germans cases are known where the confederate chieftainship, after being fairly well established, would suddenly be abolished for a while, and its powers would revert to the tribal chiefs. This may well have happened with some frequency in earlier times, as the more rigid type of chieftainship which we are discussing will hardly have been set up immutably overnight; but explicit evidence is lacking.[3]

As in the assembly so also on the battlefield the Germanic chief of either type was invested with no authority, and he had no powers of coercion. At a later date, when the Romans addressed a Germanic chief as 'king' (*basileus*), he at once repudiated the title, for the term 'king', he said, implied 'authority' while his office implied 'wisdom'. Like the other leading men, the chief in the first century A.D. would shout encouragement to his followers during the course of a battle,[4] but his

[1] Procopius, *BG* viii. 27. 23 ff.

[2] Ibid. vi. 14. 40. For the treatment of a chief of this type who did not have his people's respect see ibid. v. 11. 1, vi. 14. 11 and 39 f., 25. 23; cf. vii. 2. 10, 24. 27 and 29; Greg. Tur., *HF* iv. 14; *Heimskringla: St Olav* lxxx.

[3] Bede, *HE* iv. 12 *init.*; Procopius, *BG* vi. 14. 38; Paul. Diac., *HL* ii. 32. Whether a child could succeed in Tacitus' time is unknown: for later periods see Amm. Marc. xxxi. 3. 3; Procopius, *BV* iii. 3. 24, *BG* v. 2. 1, vii. 35. 17, viii. 27. 19.

[4] Tacitus, *A* ii. 15. 2. There is a good note on a typical Germanic chief (Fulcaris the Herul) in Agathias, *Hist.* i. 14. For the rejection of the title 'king' by the Visigoth Athanaric see Themistius, *Or.* x. 134 D.

position seems to have been of a purely moral character: he could only set an example and advise,[1] though neither his example nor his advice might attract much attention from the warriors.[2] In war as in peace the power wielded by a German chief was not inherent in his office but depended for the most part on his personal ascendancy and on the influence which his personal qualities enabled him to bring to bear. Though Roman interference with a Germanic community might result in the chief's acquiring coercive power of a formal and decisive character (p. 93 f. below), he had not such power in normal circumstances: he could not impose his wishes on the warriors. Thus, when Arminius had a Roman army at his mercy in A.D. 15 the Cherusci refused to adopt the tactics which he recommended as their military leader, and instead preferred to follow the advice of Arminius' father's brother Inguiomerus. The plan of the forthcoming battle was discussed among the leading men, and the tactical scheme which Arminius suggested was overruled in spite of the enormous prestige which he must have enjoyed at this date.[3] Segestes even threw Arminius into chains at a time, apparently, when Arminius was the military chieftain of the Cherusci (perhaps in the period A.D. 9–15).[4] Finally, the powers of life and death which the chief is said to have

---

[1] Tacitus, *G* vii. 1 f., xi. 5 f.; cf. *A* ii. 15. 2, 17. 5. See esp. V. Grönbech, *The Culture of the Teutons* (London and Copenhagen, 1931), i, 159–74.

[2] Tacitus, *G* vi. 6, *A* ii. 14. 5. But Adam of Bremen, cited on p. 34 n. 1 above, continues: 'itaque domi pares esse gaudent, in prelium euntes omnem prebent obedientiam regi vel ei qui doctior ceteris a rege prefertur', which is hardly true of Tacitus' Germans.

[3] Tacitus, *A* i. 68. 1; cf. 57. 1 'validiore apud eos Arminio, quoniam bellum suadebat'—not because he was their elected leader; Velleius, ii. 118. 3 'opprimi posse Romanos et dicit et persuadet' (sc. Arminius in A.D. 9).

[4] Tacitus, *A* i. 58. 5 (though *vincire* was illegal except for the priests: *G* vii. 2). This is not incredible, cf. the references on p. 36 n. 2 above.

possessed over his followers in wartime in Caesar's day had passed from him and had been taken over by the priests, who could also coerce the people into silence when they gathered for a meeting of the assembly.[1] But in Caesar's time the priests, if they existed, were of so little significance that he makes no mention of them at all; and several of the functions of the priests in Tacitus' day had been discharged by holy women in Caesar's time and earlier.[2] There had undoubtedly been a rapid growth in the powers of the priests just as there had been a rapid growth in the anthropomorphism of their religion and in the individualizing of their gods in the interval between Caesar and Tacitus.[3] But the chiefs could not parallel the priests' acquisition of coercive power.

Many questions about the powers and functions of the chiefs cannot be answered. Did those chiefs who held office in peacetime have any say in deciding which part of the people's land should be brought under cultivation each year and in distributing it 'according to social standing' (p. 18 above)? Had the idea made any headway that the land in some sense belonged to them? To what extent were they held responsible for the failure of the crops? What were their priestly or magical powers, if any? There can be no answer; but there are two other points which should be observed. The multi-

---

[1] Id., *G* vii. 2, xi. 4. See p. 13 n. 1 above. For the priests see Chadwick, art. cit. (on p. 32 n. 2 above), 268–300.

[2] Id., *Origin of the English Nation* (Cambridge, 1907), 317 f. The first known German priest is mentioned in Strabo, vii. 1. 4.

[3] Contrast Caesar, *BG* vi. 21. 2 with Tacitus, *G* ix, and note the deliberate attempt of Civilis to build up Veleda's influence so that she might have more power over his German followers, id., *H* iv. 65 *fin.*, though there is no parallel in early Germanic history to the Dacian kings' political use of religion, for which see the historian Crito, 200 F 7 (Jacoby). For new evidence about Veleda see *L'année épigraphique* (1953), 13 f., with references, and P.-W. viii A, 620 f.

plicity of war-chiefs which was usual in Caesar's time and which is still found among the fourth-century Burgundians and Franks (p. 14 above) has in general disappeared. But the tendency to appoint dual commanders, of which we found an example even in the middle of the first century B.C., has now grown widespread. It would be a mistake to suppose that only one of these couples was an army leader and that the other was a sort of remote 'priest-king', for several cases are known where both alike took the field together at the head of their people's levy. Although this dual command does not occur among those peoples who had a 'royal clan', it is found frequently among the other peoples in and after the first century A.D.;[1] and no case is known from early Germany where the old free institutions were overthrown and a tyranny established by a military chief who had a colleague of equal standing with himself. Indeed, it may be that the people appointed the two war-chiefs with equal power and rank precisely in order to prevent the domination of a single man even in their military affairs. Secondly, it may be that Tacitus has oversimplified his picture of the Germanic chieftainship: at any rate, there is nothing in his

---

[1] Tacitus, *A* xii. 30. 4, xiii. 54. 2, *H* iii. 5 (cf. 21 *fin.*); Dio Cassius, lxxi. 12. 1; Dexippus, 100 F 7 § 2 (Jacoby), where the Vandals in the third century have two kings and also a number of ἄρχοντες, some at least of whom were οὐ μάλα πόρρω ἀξιώσεως. For other examples see *Paneg. Lat.* iv (x). 16. 5 f., vi (vii). 11. 5 (cf. p. 13 n. 2 above); Amm. Marc. xvi. 12. 23; Jordanes, *Get.* liv. 277; Paul. Diacon. i. 7; Willibald, *Vita Bonifatii* vi (p. 26, ed. Levison); etc. See further E. A. Thompson, *Nottingham Medieval Studies*, v (1961), 21 n. 85, and below p. 99 n. 1. These cases must be distinguished from e.g. that of the seventh-century East Saxons who also on occasion had two kings; but these two kings, at any rate *c.* 664, divided the people into two parts and ruled the two parts independently and with very different policies: see Bede, *HE* iii. 30 (who refers elsewhere to several cases of dual kingship). There is no parallel to this territorial division among the Germans of the Roman period except when they had entered the Imperial provinces.

pages so complex as the system which existed among the Alamanni in the middle of the fourth century. At the battle of Strasbourg in 357 the Alamannic warriors were led by two confederate chiefs, Chonodomarius and his brother's son Serapio, who are not known to have held any exceptional position in time of peace.[1] Subordinate to these were five 'kings nearest in power' to them,[2] and an unknown number of similar 'kings' (*reges*) took no part in the campaign: these were the leaders of the tribes (*pagi*). Under the five *reges* stood ten 'petty kings' (*regales*) whose powers and functions are unknown.[3] Finally, our authority tells how one of the *reges* invited to a banquet 'all the *reges* and *regales* and *reguli*' in his neighbourhood,[4] though without mentioning the difference between the *regales* and the *reguli*. Similarly, among the fourth-century Quadi we hear of a *rex*, a *regalis*, and a *subregulus* as well as optimates and judges.[5]

An elective office implies electors. The electors in Germanic society were no doubt the assembled warriors. Presumably the council of the leading men after discussing the matter among themselves over their mead, their beer, or more probably their imported wine, would nominate a candidate to the assembly, which would then express its approval or disapproval.[6] The candi-

---

[1] Amm. Marc. xvi. 12. 23.

[2] Ibid. 26 'potestate proximi reges'.

[3] Ibid. The only Alamannic *regalis* known by name is Rando, ibid. xxvii. 10. 1 f., who was evidently able to undertake a raid on the Roman provinces without reference to any higher Alamannic authority.

[4] Ibid. xviii. 2. 13; cf. *SHA, Probus*, xiv. 2 *reguli novem*.

[5] Ibid. xvii. 12. 21. For the clan-chieftainship among the fourth-century Burgundians see Dessau, *ILS* 2813. 'Hariulfus protector domesitigus filius Hanhavaldi, regalis gentis Burgundionum, qui vicxit annos xx et mensses nove et dies nove. Reudilo avunculus ipsius fecit'.

[6] Tacitus, *G* xxii. 3 'de . . . adsciscendis principibus . . . in conviviis consultant', though if this is how the words are to be interpreted, we

date nominated by the leading men would almost invariably be one of themselves (as was obligatory in the case of the eighth-century Saxons),[1] though in a community where a 'royal clan' existed they would have no choice but to nominate one of its members—it would probably not even occur to them to do otherwise. There is no indication that there existed in the times of Caesar and Tacitus any machinery for peaceably deposing a chief when once he had been elected. But if a chief became detached from the people, became haughty and ambitious, and no longer interpreted their wishes loyally, he might eventually find himself expelled not only from his office but also from the people's territory.[2] But the assassination of an unpopular chief was an event of the greatest rarity; and we may suspect that the people would endure a long period of misrule and injustice before they would take so drastic a step as even to expel their properly constituted leader from their territory (p. 86 below).[3]

The third great force in Germanic society besides the council of the leading men and the war-chieftainship was the general assembly of the warriors, from which none was excluded except the warrior who had thrown away his shield in battle.[4] It is not known how often the assembly met. It ordinarily met at certain fixed times throughout the year when the moon was new or full; but special meetings could be called in times of emergency.[5]

should expect *ducibus* or *regibus* instead of *principibus*. But Tacitus, of course, is not consistent or rigorous in the use of technical terms.

[1] Bede, *HE* v. 10.

[2] e.g. Tacitus, *A* xii. 29. 1; see pp. 86, 88 below. Observe that in Procopius, *BG* vi. 14. 11 ff., there is no question of deposing Rodulf.

[3] For two examples of assassination (the second inspired by Roman intrigue) see Amm. Marc. xvi. 12. 17; Claudian, *i cons. Stil.* 243.

[4] Tacitus, *G* vi. 6.

[5] Ibid. xi. 2 'nisi quid fortuitum et subitum incidit', and in the case of the Saxons such meetings were observed by Charlemagne, *Capit. de Part.*

No doubt the frequency of ordinary meetings will have varied somewhat from people to people, and within the one people meetings were probably held more often in times of war and crisis than in time of peace. Thus, in 180 the Emperor Commodus ordered the Marcomanni to meet not more often than once a month (p. 103 below); and the inference would seem to be that in a time of unsuccessful warfare, hardship, and devastation the Marcomannic assembly had been meeting with great frequency, which is understandable when the tribesmen were almost continuously assembled for purposes of war.[1] Among some modern peoples cases are known where the assembly meets at very short intervals, at times almost weekly, even in peacetime: normally only the men in the capital attend these meetings, but on important occasions this is not so.[2] Accordingly, there is no reason to doubt the frequency of the Marcomannic assemblies in wartime. Among that same people there were several different places where the warriors might gather; and some at least of the Germanic peoples would meet in a sacred wood.[3] In exceptional times the as-

*Saxon.* xviii 'ut in dominicis diebus conventus et placita publica non faciant nisi forte pro magna necessitate aut hostilitate cogente'.

[1] Dio Cassius, lxxii. 2. 4. Observe that in the eighth century the Saxon council normally met only once a year: *Vita Lebuini Antiqua* iv 'morisque erat ut semel in anno generale consilium agerent in media Saxonia iuxta fluvium Wisuram [ = Weser] ad locum qui dicitur Marklo . . . renovabant ibi leges [would this be true of Tacitus' Germans?], praecipuas causas adiudicabant et quid per annum essent acturi sive in bello sive in pace communi consilio statuebant'. As for the composition of this council the *Vita* goes on: 'solebant ibi omnes in unum satrapae [i.e. leaders of *pagi*] convenire, ex pagis quoque singulis duodecim electi nobiles totidemque liberi totidemque lati'. There is no hint in our sources of such a representative principle among any of the Germanic peoples of the Roman period. The nearest approach to it would seem to be the curious Marcomannic embassy which negotiated with Commodus in 180 (p. 46 below). Cf. Tacitus, *G* xxxix. 2 *legationibus*.

[2] M. Fortes and E. E. Evans-Pritchard, *African Political Systems* (Oxford, 1940), 72.

[3] Dio Cassius, loc. cit.; Tacitus, *A* ii. 12. 1, *H* iv. 14.

sembly might take on a somewhat less formal aspect than it normally wore. When Civilis decided to revolt against the Romans in A.D. 69 it might have been disastrous to send messengers throughout the people summoning the warriors to come and discuss the proposal, for it was essential that his intentions should be kept secret. What he did was to invite the leading men of the Batavians together with the most forward of the rank-and-file warriors to a sacred grove on the pretext of holding a feast. When the merriment was at its height he put his proposals before the feasters, who greeted his words with applause and bound themselves with an oath. In this case, then, the assembly, if it may be so called—for in fact it was something more than a council of the leading men and something less than a general assembly of all the warriors—was summoned on the personal initiative of Civilis, and he alone addressed it. But the case is exceptional, for the Batavians were incorporated in the Empire, and it was essential to the success of Civilis' plans of revolt that the decision should not become known to the Romans. It cannot be supposed that this procedure was often adopted in free Germany, even in the case of extraordinary meetings.[1] A form of procedure which may have been less unusual is recorded from A.D. 15. In that year the decision of the Cherusci to resist the advance of Germanicus' legions was not taken at a formal assembly at all. There would not have been time to summon one; and so the military chief Arminius hurried from settlement to settlement, and with his fiery words roused the people to take up arms in defence of their freedom, their homes, and their traditional ways.[2] We do not know whether the council had given him authority to do this.

[1] Id., *H* iv. 14 f.          [2] Id., *A* i. 59. 2 ff.

In spite of the growing inequalities of economic power and social standing among the Germans of the first century A.D. this assembly of the free tribesmen was still in some sense the sovereign body. It is true that the assembly could not initiate measures, and there is no evidence that anyone other than the 'king' (*rex*) in societies where there was a royal clan, and one of the leading men in societies where there was no royal clan, could put a proposal before the warriors. Indeed, there is no conclusive evidence that anyone else could even address the assembly formally.[1] If we may be guided by evidence which dates from a much later period[2] we might suppose the procedure to have been this: if the proposal put forward by the chief were generally applauded there would be no further discussion, and this was the case when Civilis addressed the Batavian assembly in A.D. 69. But if the proposal led to an obvious division of opinion, then one or perhaps more than one of the leading men might speak and try to reinforce the chief's arguments. But no rank-and-file warrior would deliver a speech on his own account. There is no reason to think that there could be a formal debate, or that a common warrior could eloquently criticize the chief's proposal, demolishing it point by point. The assembly could do no more than adopt or reject the proposals put before it by the military leader or one of the leading men; but its decision was final.[3]

In the majority of cases its decision must have been reached more or less unanimously, for there were no

---

[1] Unless, of course, we read *principes* in Tacitus, *G* xi. 5.

[2] In the Swedish assembly at Birca in 852, when the *rex* put forward a controversial proposal and the people 'diversa sentire et tumultuare coeperunt', then 'unus qui erat senior natu' got up and spoke at length: Rimbertus, *Vita S. Anskarii* xxvii (p. 58).

[3] Tacitus, *G* xi. 1 and 5–6.

peaceable means by which a substantial minority of the people could have been coerced into a course of action of which they strongly disapproved: there was even in Tacitus' time no public and coercive authority over and above the people themselves. It is true that a fundamental cleavage of opinion arose among the Chatti at some date earlier than Caesar's day; and the result was that the dissidents migrated in a body and became a separate and independent people called the Batavians. It is unthinkable that the dissidents could have been kept at home and compelled to accept the decision of their opponents.[1] In general, however, when class differences were in so rudimentary a stage, there will not normally have been any insuperable difficulty in agreeing more or less unanimously on a proposed course of action. It has been said of many a primitive society that 'it seems very rare for opinions to be in conflict in such an assembly. It is indeed surprising to what an extent the people's ways of thinking in public affairs run along identical lines, and the same unanimity is apparent when the general opinion is to be put into practice'. But it is surprising only if we forget that social classes or groups with conflicting interests have not yet evolved in such societies.[2] On the other hand, even in the first century A.D., as the clan system decayed in western Germany and internal conflicts began to develop, we hear of persons 'who have no hope save through dissensions' and 'who flourished on factions'.[3]

[1] Ibid. xxix. 1, *H* iv. 12. Note the absence of any reference to coercion in the Vandal legend reported by Procopius, *BV* iii. 22. 3.

[2] Landtman, op. cit. (on p. 25 n. 1 above), 310, cf. 315 f. In the vivid scene depicted by Rimbertus, op. cit. xxviii, the final decision was reached 'omnium unanima voluntate et consensu'; and note ibid. xxvi *unanimi*, quoted on p. 35 n. 2 above.

[3] Tacitus, *A* xi. 16. 5, 17. 4, both referring to the Cherusci at a time when the old system of government had seriously decayed.

It is a pity that nothing is known of the identity of these men or of how they set to work.

What business came before the assembly? It certainly had the right to decide whether to declare war or to conclude peace. The embassies sent by the Marcomanni to Marcus Aurelius late in the second century are frequently mentioned, but our authority never says that they were sent by the chief: it was the people who sent them and whom they represented on each occasion.[1] Sometimes, indeed, the clans would negotiate separately each on its own account (p. 11 n. 2 above), or the embassy sent by the people might be composed of the military leader and one representative of each of the ten tribes of which the Marcomanni were composed.[2] At a time of exceptional distress and destruction the people negotiated through two of their leading men accompanied by two rank-and-file warriors.[3] But no case is known where the chief negotiated on his own initiative and as a plenipotentiary. The assembly also exercised judicial functions in cases which were thought to affect the community as a whole. Tacitus lists treachery, desertion, cowardice, and homosexuality as examples. For

[1] Petrus Patricius, frag. 6; Dio Cassius, lxvii. 7. 1, lxxi. 11. 3, 15. 1, 20. 1, lxxii. 2. 1. Observe that the Alamanni of Vadomarius' *pagus* joined in the invasion of Gaul in 357 although Vadomarius himself afterwards claimed that he had opposed participation: Amm. Marc. xvi. 12. 17 (assuming that Clark's text gives the sense of what Ammianus wrote). It seems unlikely that Vadomarius would have invented such an excuse, which reflected on his own prestige, if in fact his people had not had the right to overrule him in the matter of going to war. Similarly, the Alamannic chief does not conclude peace on his own initiative, ibid. xiv. 10. 9. Neither Tacitus, *G* xxii. 3, nor Amm. Marc. xxviii. 5. 10, warrants us in believing that the *principes* or the *reges* had the right to decide on war or peace without reference to the assembly.

[2] Petrus Patricius, loc. cit.

[3] Dio Cassius, lxxii. 2. 1. A century later the Vandals negotiated with Aurelian through their chiefs and their leading men: Dexippus, 100 F 7 § 2 (Jacoby). See also E. A. Thompson, *Nottingham Medieval Studies*, v (1961), 22, on the Visigoths.

all such offences against the community the punishment was death: these were offences which could not be compounded for.[1] It is also noteworthy that Tacitus insists that no free warrior could be bound, whipped, or beaten by his fellows, and this immunity was drastically altered only after the establishment of the first Germanic States in Gaul in the fifth century.[2] It is not easy to say what other kinds of business were transacted by the assembly in addition to its election of chiefs and judges, its discussion of questions of war and peace, and its judicial functions. But no doubt other matters arose, too: for example, the decision of the Suebi to prohibit the import of wine into their territory was doubtless an assembly decision.[3]

We have now discussed the evidence relating to the three great organs of government of the people as a whole.[4] Throughout our discussion we found it difficult to say which of the three was the decisive political force in each community. It was certainly not the confederate leader, for in circumstances calling for decisions of critical importance he could be flatly overruled by the optimates (p. 37 above). Nor was it the council of the optimates, for at meetings of the assembly the final decision lay not with them but with the rank and file of the warriors, whose own powers, however, were severely restricted by the fact that they could not formally initiate any policy, though they could block any

[1] Tacitus, *G* xii. 1; but contrast xxxi. 2. See L. T. Hobhouse, G. C. Wheeler, and M. Ginsberg, *The Material Culture and Social Institutions of the Simpler Peoples* (London, 1930), 55.
[2] But the priests had some such powers: Tacitus, *G* vii. 2.
[3] Caesar, *BG* iv. 2. 6.
[4] On village life see E. A. Thompson, *Historia*, iv (1955), 331–8. There is no evidence for 'thousands' or 'hundreds' at this date: H. G. Gundel, *Untersuchungen zur Taktik und Strategie der Germanen nach den antiken Quellen*, Diss. Marburg (1937), 21 f.; H. Dannenbauer, *Histor. Jahrbuch*, lxii–lxix (1942–9), 155 ff.; and others.

policy proposed by the chief and the council. The fact is that society was still so primitive, so undifferentiated, that it is misleading to regard the three organs of government as being in any significant or permanent way opposed to one another. The chief, the leading men, and the common warriors were not three distinct and hostile bodies, for there were few or no interests to divide them. The three organs of government were not the political weapons of three opposing classes. In the time of Tacitus, however, there was a further institution which was destined to play a prominent part in destroying or transforming all three organs of government alike.

## 2. *The Retinues*

With the accumulation of privately owned wealth a blow had been struck at the clan as the basic unit of society (pp. 18 ff. above). This change put more wealth into private hands and so in its turn helped to bring about a social innovation which was of fundamental importance. This innovation concerned the 'retinue' (*comitatus*).

In the middle of the first century B.C. one of the leading men of a people would announce in the assembly of the warriors that he proposed to undertake a raid or foray; and he would there and then call for followers. It was not necessary for him to secure the assent of the council or the assembly for his enterprise. The mere announcement of it would furnish a practical test of its popularity. Whoever was attracted by the raid and the leader would volunteer his services, and once he had done so the force of public opinion would not allow him to withdraw.[1] Now, two facts should be noted in this

[1] Caesar, *BG* vi. 23. 7 f.

procedure. In the first place, the relationship between the leader and the follower was a purely temporary one, lasting only for the duration of the foray. The follower could in no way be described as a dependent of the leader, and indeed it may be doubted whether the leader could exercise any real authority over those whom he led: such power would have been anomalous in Germanic society at that date.[1] The implication of Caesar's words is that the band would disperse as soon as it returned home from its raid. It was an *ad hoc* body and nothing more. A few days or a few weeks would see both its beginning and its end. Secondly, in such expeditions there was little room for the kindred, which was the unit of the levy when the whole host of the people was called out for war; for some members of the clan might volunteer to take part in the raid while others might not. The fact that one member of a kinship-group set off with the raiding party imposed no obligation on the other members of it to go with him. As a consequence of this the booty taken on such expeditions would tend to widen differences of wealth not only in the community in question but even inside the clans themselves, for there is no reason to suppose that on their return home the different members of the raiding party would share the spoils—primarily cattle, slaves, and jewelry—with their kinsmen.[2] In the days of Caesar, then, these private raids carried out by a leader and his

---

[1] For what they are worth see Dudo, *De moribus Normanniae ducum* ii (Migne, *PL* cxli, 639), where the Franks say to Rollo's band of raiding Normans, ' "quo nomine vester senior fungitur?" responderunt, "nullo, quia aequalis potestatis sumus" ', Sidonius, *Ep.* viii. 6. 13 (on the Saxon sea-raiders): 'quot remiges videris, totidem te cernere putes archipiratas: ita simul omnes imperant parent, docent discunt latrocinari'.

[2] Wine and food taken as booty would tend to be consumed more or less on the spot: Tacitus, *A* xii. 27. 4; Zosimus, iv. 23. 4, 25. 2; Paul. Diacon., *HL* v. 5; cf. Willibald, *Vita S. Bonifatii* viii (pp. 50 f., ed. Levison); etc.

retinue undoubtedly tended to increase differences of wealth inside the clans and were to that extent a disruptive element in Germanic society as it existed at that time.

Now in the period of which Tacitus speaks the institution of the retinue had become very different. The leader of the retinue had in the meantime transformed his relationship with his 'companions' (*comites*) into something like a permanent one. Although he did not reward them with grants of land—for he still *owned* no land which he might have given them[1]—yet he supplied them with their military equipment, including so valuable an item as their warhorses. He fed them and kept them about him not only in wartime and during the raids which he organized but also in time of peace; and the greater the number of 'companions' whom he was able to support, the higher was his prestige in his community. Instead of being a purely temporary arrangement lasting only for the duration of a single raid, the retinue had now taken on a far more permanent character and was in full process of revolutionizing Germanic society. When such a retinue went out to war along with the forces of the people as a whole, the men included in it would not fight side by side with their own kinsmen but would fight shoulder to shoulder with the other warriors who composed the retinue to which they belonged. If their leader were taken prisoner or if he went into banishment or were killed, they would voluntarily share his captivity or his exile or his doom.[2] And

---

[1] Observe the absence of reference to land in *Cod. Euric.* 310 f., though cf. *Legg. Visig.* v. 3. 4. The first Germanic leaders who presented land to some of their favoured followers were the Burgundian kings: *Legg. Burg.* i. 4, xxxviii. 6. Throughout the whole of the Roman period we never hear of the administration of a region or a village being given by a *princeps* or a *rex* to one of his *comites*.

[2] Tacitus, *G* xiv. 1; Amm. Marc. xvi. 12. 60; Agathias, *Hist.* i. 15. Exile: pp. 80, 99 f. below.

what is even more important, each retinue would tend to follow and obey its own leader rather than the people's elected military chieftain, with results that we shall see (pp. 80, 82 below).

In the most primitive agricultural societies tillage is usually the work of women, while the men hunt and look after such animals as have been domesticated.[1] But after the introduction of the horse-drawn plough the work of tillage is normally transferred to the men; and it was the men who did at least the heavier work in the fields among the Germans of Tacitus' day.[2] Those chiefs who maintained a retinue, however, reverted to the old practice, but now they did not even hunt very much, though hunting still provided a part of the food-supply of the population as a whole (p. 5 above). When not engaged on one of their forays they would sleep and eat and lounge idly about while the womenfolk, the children, and the old men looked to the fields and the running of their homes.[3] Indeed, among the Chatti the bravest warriors do not seem to have had even this tenuous connexion with the business of production. They are said to have owned no houses and to have worked no land but to have been wholly supported by the rest of the population (though how in that case they

[1] G. Thomson, *Studies in Ancient Greek Society* (London, 1949), i, 42, with references. For ancient examples see Strabo, ii. 4. 7; Silius Italicus, iii. 350 ff.; etc. Some also cite Poseidonius, 87 F 58 (Jacoby), but what that fragment shows is Ligurian men and women hiring themselves out to work side by side in the fields of those who hired them. This is a very different thing: the farm labourer, whether male or female, is a much later phenomenon than societies where men have not yet begun to engage in agriculture at all.

[2] Cf. R. Hachmann, *Archaeologia Geographica* v (1956), 9 *b fin.*

[3] It would be absurd to suppose that Tacitus, *G* xiv. 4—xv. 1, refers to German men in general and to think that all the adult male population of Germany was comprised of loungers and ne'er do weels: the chiefs and their *comites* are still the subject of discussion, cf. xlvi. 1 *torpor procerum.*

maintained their retinues is not clear).[1] That is to say, even in the first century A.D. many of the leading men of the Germanic peoples had largely detached themselves from the business of production altogether except in so far as war itself had become a method of appropriation: they were in process of forming themselves into a leisured class.

What was the economic basis of this new form of the retinues? How did the leader find the means to support his companions? In the first place, both he and they owned herds of cattle which may have been larger than had been usual in Caesar's day, and they also received the produce of the fields which were worked by their slaves.[2] In the time of Caesar, when the clan lands were worked collectively, the institution of the retinue could scarcely have arisen in this form. It is unlikely that in those communal conditions the clansmen and women would have toiled to keep a minority of their able-bodied members in permanent idleness. This new type of un-productive life for a comparatively small number of the warriors only became possible when the old communal practices had been broken down and when the produce of the arable belonged to the individual. Since their share of the arable was now disproportionately large (p. 18 above) it is difficult to see how it could have been worked adequately unless they had increased the number of their slaves. At any rate, they had some surplus wealth of their own in addition to what they derived from their flocks and herds, and so were able to entertain their 'companions' at those rude but plentiful feasts of which Tacitus speaks.[3] But the productivity

[1] Ibid. xxxi. 4 f.
[2] On the omission of reference to slaves in ibid. xv. 1 see the paper cited on p. 16 n. 1 above, at p. 192 f.
[3] Ibid. xiv. 3.

of Germanic agriculture must not be exaggerated; and in fact the produce of their cattle and of the fields at their disposal was by no means enough in itself to maintain the retinues in their new form. Secondly, therefore, the leaders' means were derived from the booty taken in their raids. Raids carried out for the purpose of collecting not only prestige but also cattle, slaves, and treasure were more than ever a regular and highly respected means of passing one's life.[1] From these raids came some of the warhorses, the fine spears, and the like, with which the leaders rewarded their followers. It was the leaders' dependence on booty as an essential source of wealth which gave them some of their contempt for agricultural labour. The retinue could only be maintained if the raids were more or less continuous and if they were continuously successful; and since the fields could be tilled by the old, the women, and the children, it became a matter of shame for these chosen warriors to win by hard work in the fields what could be won by bloodshed abroad.[2] Indeed, with the acquisition of further wealth the leading men would no doubt be able to keep larger retinues, and it has been conjectured that 'the proportion of warriors [would] tend continually to increase, while the cultivation of the land was left more and more' to the women, slaves, children, etc.[3] Thirdly, in order to win the support or buy off the hostility of a famous retinue, neighbouring

---

[1] Caesar, *BG* vi. 23. 6; Mela, iii. 3; Tacitus, *G* xiv. 2, *A* xii. 29. 3.

[2] Id., *G* xiv. 4, xv. 1. Claudian, *In Eutrop.* ii. 205, makes Bellona, in the guise of Tribigild's wife, taunt him thus: 'concessoque cupit vixisse colonus quam dominus rapto . . . tolerabis iniquam pauperiem cum tela geras?'

[3] H. M. Chadwick, *Origin of the English Nation* (Cambridge, 1907), 170 f., whose view I have modified in one important respect. He thinks that agriculture was increasingly left to subject populations; but see p. 69 below.

peoples would send costly gifts to its leader—choice horses, arms, silver vases, ornaments, and so on—while the Romans would also send them money. Indeed, the sending of silver vases to the chiefs was an old practice on the part of the Romans even in Tacitus' day. The beautiful silver and bronze wine-service found with other objects in a grave at Hoby in the Danish island of Lolland has suggested that the practice was at least as old as the time of Augustus himself or Tiberius.[1] If these costly articles were in fact a gift from the Roman authorities to a Germanic chief, they give us some idea of how valuable and how beautiful such presents could be, and also of the enormous prestige which they must have brought to their owners.[2] Finally, it became customary among the various peoples to contribute voluntary gifts of cattle and grain to the leaders of retinues in their own communities; and these gifts, coming from the population at large, who were not included in the retinues (p. 57 below), played an important part in enabling the leaders to support their men.[3]

The institution of the retinue, then, had become very different since the time when Julius Caesar had observed it, and in three ways it worked for the overthrow of the

---

[1] K. Friis Johansen, *Nordiske Fortidsminder*, ii, 3 (Copenhagen, 1923), 159–64.

[2] Tacitus, *G* v. 4 *argentea vasa*, xiii. 4, xv. 3, where *phalerae torquesque* may include Roman military decorations given to the leaders of German retinues who served with the Imperial armies; cf. *A* ii. 9. 5, *H* iv. 29 *insignibus*, and for a later period Zosimus, iv. 40. 8. In the inscription of M. Valerius Maximianus published by H. G. Pflaum, *Libyca* iii (1955), 135–54 = *AE* (1956), 124 (1959), 183, we hear of the *phalerae* of Valao, *dux Naristarum*. What sort of person is denoted by *singulis* in Tacitus, *G* xv. 3? Indutiomarus and his kinsmen also offered money to the German *civitates* beyond the Rhine in the winter of 55–54 B.C., Caesar, *BG* v. 55. 1, vi. 2. 1: did that money go to the leaders of retinues? If so, was the type of retinue described by Tacitus coming into existence even in Caesar's day?

[3] Tacitus, *G* xv. 2.

old social system. In the first place, the leader of the
retinue was in some measure independent of the will of
his kinsmen and even of the assembly of the warriors. It
is true that his wealth would bring only a limited rise in
his standard of living, for the number and variety of the
luxuries and comforts which he could buy were not very
great, though their prestige-value was undoubtedly
high. It is also true that wealth consisting of herds of
cattle would not enable him to exploit directly the
labour of many of his followers or of the rank and file of
his people. It is true, too, that he might well incur the
enmity of other retinue-leaders inside or outside his own
community, who might wish to rob him of his prestige
or to avenge a wrong inflicted by him. Nonetheless, his
ability to increase the number of his dependents gave
him a more or less organized force over which his
kindred and the assembly exercised little or no control.
Indeed, the assembly might not even know how many
'companions' he had in his following at any one time:
that was a point which he might or might not disclose in
the assembly.[1] Unfortunately, we have no figures to
indicate the size of a Germanic retinue until we hear
that the Alamannic Chonodomarius in 357 had 200
warriors attending him.[2] We do not know if any
German in Tacitus' day could have supported so large a
retinue as this; and it is one of many indications of the
far greater concentration of wealth in Gaul than in
Germany that in 56 B.C. the Aquitanian Adiatunnus
fought with no fewer than 600 *soldurii*, as such retainers

[1] In 57 B.C. the Remi were able to tell Caesar (*BG* ii. 4. 4) 'quantam
quisque multitudinem in communi Belgarum concilio ad id bellum
pollicitus sit': that they were able to tell him is regarded as noteworthy.

[2] Amm. Marc. xvi. 12. 60. But this *comitatus* may have suffered casualties, and, if so, it originally numbered more than 200. In *Heimskringla:
Olaf the Quiet*, iv, we learn that Olaf (1069–93) was criticized for suppor-
ting 240 persons.

were called in Aquitania.[1] But although the assembly
did not control the retinue-leader, the activities of the
latter might well bring ruin on his fellow-tribesmen; for
his raids on neighbouring peoples would be bound
sooner or later to bring retaliatory raids in which he
himself would not necessarily suffer though many of his
people would certainly be ruined. Or if raids carried out
by one or more retinues were severely repulsed by the
enemy, the people might feel themselves obliged for
reasons of prestige to call out the general levy so as to
avenge the defeat of their leaders.[2] But the dangers
which he invited by his activities abroad were small in
comparison with the danger which he himself constituted at home. For although, as Tacitus says,[3] the
leader fought for victory, and his 'companions' fought
for their leader, it by no means followed that either
would necessarily fight for the people in general: the
victory for which they fought might well be their own
private victory directly opposed to the interests of their
people (pp. 80, 82 below). Moreover, not only was
the leader of the retinue freeing himself from the will of
the people, but persons outside the territory of his own
people were coming to regard him as an independent
force in his society. Even in peacetime foreign peoples,
as we have mentioned, would sometimes deal not with
the elected chiefs or with the assemblies but directly
with the leaders of retinues, whose prowess and powerful
following had won them a reputation beyond their own
frontiers. If a foreign people sent gifts collectively to the
head of a famous retinue so as to induce him to direct
his unwelcome attentions elsewhere (p. 53 f. above), the
gifts must have been of very considerable value, for they

---

[1] Caesar, *BG* iii. 22. 1–3.
[2] Cf. Tacitus, *A* xii. 28. 1.      [3] *G* xiv. 1.

would have to provide adequate compensation for the booty which the retinue might otherwise have collected. These gifts would strengthen the head of a retinue over against his own people by adding to his prestige, by enabling him to increase the number of his 'companions', and so on.

Secondly, the retinue was essentially an institution of the tribal nobility, and the 'companions' were usually the sons of nobles; and they fought as cavalry rather than as infantry.[1] With the means of subsistence available to the leading men of the Germanic communities in Tacitus' time there must have been a severe limit to the number of 'companions' whom a leading man could support. He would certainly not have welcomed all comers to join his ranks; and the poorer type of warrior with a small allotment of land, a man whose household was not sufficient to till his land and tend his cattle if he himself were away from home for long, will have had little chance of acceptance into the ranks of a retinue and little desire to set off on a prolonged and distant expedition. By the nature of things the retinue was aristocratic. Those, then, whom the retinues tended to free from the control of the assembly were the nobility. In a word, the retinues were in some measure a guarantee of the position of the wealthy over against the clansmen in general. In this, however, they were not always successful in the first century A.D., and on more than one recorded occasion the retinue was not able to protect its leader against the hostility of the warriors at large, and had to accompany him into exile (pp. 80, 99 f. below).

---

[1] Ibid. xiii. 2; cf. xiv. 2 f. Among the Celts of Gaul, on the other hand, the *comites* were poor freemen, Diod. Sic., v. 29. 2, so that the institution was an essentially different thing in Gaul from what it was in Germany.

Thirdly, the retinue cut across the boundaries of the various peoples altogether: a retinue was not an internal affair of the Cherusci or the Chatti or any other single people. The fame of a successful leader would attract young noblemen from neighbouring peoples; and, on the other hand, if a community remained at peace for any considerable period, there might be an exodus of young nobles, who would seek out the wars which were going on elsewhere, thus denuding their own people of a number of their best-equipped warriors. The retinue, in fact, cut across the boundaries of people and people, and took on an 'international' character.[1] Moreover, the leaders of the retinues began to adopt customs which, although common to themselves, were not shared by the warriors as whole. For example, the burial customs and practices of a number of the leading men and their womenfolk from the lower Elbe and Saale eastwards almost as far as the Vistula took on to some extent a different form from those of the rank and file of the peoples who lived in that region; and this new form, which could be found from Hanover to Poland and from Denmark to Silesia, was an 'international' one. These graves are marked by a profusion of valuable Roman luxury goods, and their character tends not to vary as between the chiefs of the several peoples but to be common to the chiefs irrespective of what people they lived among. 'Their astonishing uniformity', it has been said, 'indicates something more than chance. Their furniture shows us a well-to-do society intertribal in scope and shaped by uniform conventions and aspirations', a society sharply distinguished from that of the

---

[1] Tacitus, *G* xiv. 2; cf. e.g. Bede, *HE* iii. 14 'et undique ad eius [King Oswine's] ministerium de cunctis prope provinciis viri etiam nobilissimi concurrerent'.

common warriors.[1] Scarcely unconnected with this uniformity of custom among the leading men in many parts
of Germany is the tendency for weapons to become
standardized in the first two centuries A.D. Hitherto
weapons had shown strong local variations, but in these
centuries the variations tended to die away, and more or
less uniform types of weapon came to be used throughout the Germanic world.[2] Again, the nobility of the
various peoples would on occasion intermarry. One of
the wives of Ariovistus was not a German at all but a
Celt from Noricum. Later on, Sesithacus, the son of one
of the leading men of the Cherusci, married a woman
named Ramis, the daughter of one of the leading men
of the Chatti; and Arminius' brother Flavus also married the daughter of a chieftain of the Chatti.[3]

In these three ways, then, the retinue of the first
century A.D. worked against the solidarity of each
people among whom it had become established: (a) it
gave the leading men an independent military power

[1] Wheeler, op. cit. (on p. 21 n. 2 above), 44 f. See esp. Eggers, op. cit.
50; cf. 45, id., *Prähistorische Zeitschrift*, xxxiv–xxxv (1949–50), 58–111,
R. Hachmann, *Archaeologia Geographica* v (1956), 17 ff. These graves date
from the century 50–150, were unknown in Caesar's time, and did not
survive the formation of the third-century confederacies: Eggers, op. cit.
63. For an English account of the Lübsow-type graves, see Wheeler, op.
cit. 32 ff. His view that they are not the graves of military leaders but of
native 'new rich' distinct from the military aristocracy is unconvincing:
there is no evidence for the existence of such a class. The absence of
weapons from the graves does not prove that these people lived a peaceful
life, op. cit. 34. If it did, archaeology could prove that the Visigoths were
a peaceful people with no warleaders, for they hardly ever buried
weapons with their dead.

[2] M. Jahn, *Die Bewaffnung der Germanen in der älteren Eisenzeit* (Leipzig,
1916), 10.

[3] Caesar, *BG* i. 53. 4; Strabo, vii. 1. 4; Tacitus, *A* xi. 16. 2; cf. 17. 2.
With the polygamy mentioned by Caesar there cf. Tacitus, *G* xviii. 1, and
even Adam of Bremen, iv. 21, speaking of the eleventh-century Swedes:
'in sola mulierum copula modum nesciunt; quisque secundum faculta-
tem suarum virium duas aut tres et amplius simul habet; divites et
principes absque numero. nam et filios ex tali coniunctione genitos
habent legitimos'.

which was not wholly subject to the control of the assembly and which might be used contrary to the assembly's interests, (b) it was more or less exclusive to the aristocracy and it separated them off from their fellow-tribesmen, and (c) in spite of their personal rivalries it provided something like a common bond which tended to give the nobility an 'international' character.

### 3. Justice and Warfare

These, then, were some of the chief features of Germanic society as it was in Caesar's time and as it had become when Tacitus wrote. The accumulation of privately owned wealth strongly favoured the patrilineal organization of the clans as against the matrilineal. The consequent inheritance of property by a man's children rather than by his kindred tended to undermine the clan altogether and to elevate the monogamous family at the expense of the clan. Moreover, differences of wealth between the individuals who were included in one and the same clan were helping to bring an hereditary nobility into being. This nobility had secured something not far removed from the private ownership of land, and it was winning for itself a position in which it could set itself free from many of the restraints with which a clan society restricts the growth of any individual's power, privilege, and prestige. These men were securing their new social position by means of an institution, the retinue, which could only have come into existence when comparatively large quantities of wealth were owned by individuals. In spite of their numerous personal feuds the optimates now had certain common interests over against the warriors at large. The tie between Inguiomerus the Cheruscan and

Maroboduus the king of the Marcomanni was closer in the end than the tie between Inguiomerus and the rest of the Cherusci (p. 82 f. below). In the general process of change the military leadership had not been unaffected. Whereas the office had hitherto been open to all the warriors, at any rate in theory, there were now peoples among whom the chieftainship was confined to the members of one clan. Power is being centralized.

Another change took place between the time of Caesar and that of Tacitus which seems to have affected the Germanic peoples generally. This concerned the administration of justice.

In Caesar's day the most prominent men of each *pagus* expounded tribal custom on disputed matters and tried to reconcile the parties (p. 10 above). But their proceedings will have been wholly informal. There is no evidence that they could compel the disputants to appear before them or that they could enforce their decisions.[1] They could only use their influence; and the weight of their influence would presumably vary according to their own personal characters and prestige and to the circumstances of the case which they were hearing. There seem to have been no means, other than the pressure of public opinion, of coercing a refractory party. Caesar does not specify what kind of case would come before these 'judges', but we may suspect that they were often concerned with the allocation of the arable, the boundaries of clan holdings, and perhaps also the ownership of cattle.

But 150 years later these 'courts' had developed and had grown less informal. The popular assembly now elected a certain number of the leading men to act as judges; and these judges travelled through the tribes

[1] See Anderson, *Germania* 90.

and villages to hear 'private' suits. (Crimes which were thought to affect the community as a whole were tried by the assembly itself.) Each of these judges was accompanied by 100 of the tribesmen to give advice and to lend authority to his decisions.[1] A party who was found guilty by them was obliged to pay a number of horses or cattle proportionate to the gravity of his offence: the precise number was fixed sometimes no doubt by custom, but often by the judge. Some of the cattle and horses were payable to the winning party or in a case of homicide to his kindred; but the remainder was payable as a fine to the chieftain or to the people. That is to say, other wrongs besides treachery, cowardice, and so on (p. 46 above), were now coming to be regarded as no longer merely private wrongs but as offences which in some measure affected the community as a whole.[2] On the other hand, although the hundred companions of the judge could lend weight to his decision, there is no reason to suppose that they could compel an unwilling party to accept it, especially if that party were a powerful member of the nobility. Indeed, there is no evidence that they could even force an unwilling party to appear before them at all. Cases of homicide, for example, seem in Tacitus' time to have been dealt with more often by the kindreds than by those leading men who were elected to dispense justice. In fact, however, the decisions of primitive courts are in general obeyed readily, so great is the power of public opinion,[3] which among the Cherusci forced even the influential Segestes to fight against the Romans whom

[1] Tacitus, *G* xii. 3.

[2] Ibid. 2. Anderson rightly takes the words 'sed et levioribus . . . exsolvitur' as 'an anticipatory parenthesis, suggested by the penalties for *delicta maiora*', and holds that private suits were not heard in the assembly.

[3] A. S. Diamond, *Primitive Law* (London, 1950), 197 f.

he supposed to be the champions and guarantors of his social position among his people (p. 75 below). But as primitive societies divide up into classes, and the interests of members are no longer identical, then the power of public opinion declines: the people no longer speak with one united voice. And it is noteworthy that while Germanic judges appear to have acted alone in the time of Caesar, they were each accompanied by a small army of 100 men in Tacitus' day so as to reinforce the strength of public opinion. Moreover, whereas in Caesar's time the chiefs of the various tribes settled disputes among their own tribesmen (p. 10 above) or at any rate attempted to do so, this was no longer the case in the time referred to by Tacitus. The judges were now elected by a central body, the assembly of the warriors, and not locally in the *pagus*. The warriors of any one tribe would, of course, have their place in the general assembly; but they would be outnumbered there, and their voice might not be decisive in the election of the judge who was to come and pronounce upon their affairs. The judge now came into the local community from outside, and he might well be a stranger to those among whom he was to adjudicate. In Tacitus' time the administration of justice was on the way to becoming the work of something like a centralized machine.

A remarkable change was also coming over the character of warfare in the period between Caesar and Tacitus. Tactics in general were still little different from what they had been among the Achaeans of Homer's day. There was little or no centralized direction of the fighting; and discipline, as a Roman would have understood the term, was lacking. It was still the practice to go into battle in bands composed of families and kindreds;[1] and each band tended to operate on its own initiative and without paying too much attention to any over-all tactical scheme which might or might not have been thought out beforehand. A battle might well resolve itself into a series of disconnected and sporadic assaults on the enemy's line by the various kinship-groups and retinues of which the levy was composed.[2] The chieftain's control over the warriors was slight: his function once battle had been joined was merely to encourage them by setting an example of daring and *élan*.[3] As long as their social organization remained what it was in the time of Caesar it would have been next to impossible for the Germanic leaders —indeed, it would probably have occurred to no one—to separate kinsman from kinsman in the battle-line, to break with the age-old practice, and to form the warriors into units based on some other principle than blood-relationship: what would have been gained from the change when the social division of labour was in general so primitive among them? It would have been

[1] Tacitus, *G* vii. 3; cf. the *locus classicus* on the Franks and Lombards in Mauricius, *Strateg.* xi. 4 (J. Schefferus, *Arriani Tactica* (Uppsala, 1664), 269 f.). Note also *Pactus Alamann.* ii. 45 'in heris generationis', which Lehmann, ad loc., explains as 'ante exercitum secundum familias ordinatum'. The organization in kindreds would have had little or no significance if kinship had been limited to close blood-relationship.

[2] Tacitus, *G* xxx. 3, *H* iv. 76, *A* ii. 14. 5, 45. 3; cf. Themistius, *Or.* xv. 197 B. With Tacitus, *G* vi. 6 'cedere loco, dummodo rursus instes, consilii quam formidinis arbitrantur', contrast Mauricius, *Strateg.* loc. cit., on the sixth-century Franks and Lombards: τὴν δειλίαν καὶ τὴν πρὸς μικρὸν ἀναχώρησιν εἰς ὄνειδος ἔχονται (cf. Procopius, *BG* viii. 35. 27), though Mauricius adds (p. 270): ἀπειθῆ δὲ ὄντα τοῖς ἄρχουσιν αὐτῶν, καὶ ἀπράγμονα, καὶ πάσης ποικιλίας καὶ ἀσφαλείας ἐκτὸς, καὶ τῆς τοῦ συμφέροντος γνώμης τάξεως περιφρονοῦσι, which squares with Tacitus' Homeric type of warfare. Note Wittigis' elaborate apologia for his strategic withdrawal to Ravenna in 536: Procopius, *BG* v. 11. 19 ff. But Fulcaris the Herul refused to retreat from Parma in 552 and was killed there: Agathias, *Hist.* i. 15, δεδιὼς δὴ οὖν, ὡς ἔοικε, τὴν κακηγορίαν μᾶλλον τοῦ ξίφους.

[3] Tacitus, *G* vii. 1 f., etc.

unthinkable, too, for the clansmen to give their military leader coercive powers over his fellow-warriors without a general reconstruction of the very nature of their society which would have introduced entirely new ideas of power and authority. True, Civilis seems to have thought that service in the Roman army would in itself give Germans some Roman discipline. When any of them enlisted in the Imperial army the Romans' first task was to teach them discipline as that word was understood in the Empire: the barbarian recruits were attached to a centurion who would include some Roman troops in their companies to set them an example, and so would proceed to break them in and accustom them to accept and obey orders.[1] But although service with the Romans might supply a Germanic leader with some useful strategical ideas,[2] yet Civilis' words, as reported by Tacitus, are restrained.[3] Individuals might learn something of Roman discipline, but this would not be true of the people's levy as a whole.

But the tribal system was disintegrating among some of the Germans, and so this incapacity to fight otherwise than as a free levy was on the point of being overcome by a few peoples in the first century A.D. (quite apart from the retinues). The peoples who had reached this stage of development, however, attracted the attention of the Romans and were clearly exceptional. When the Cherusci attacked Maroboduus in A.D. 17

[1] Id., *Agr.* xxviii. 2.

[2] See e.g. Caesar, *BG* iii. 23. 5 ff., which also illustrates the uselessness of such ideas when adopted by a tribal levy fighting against highly trained and well equipped forces of a far more advanced civilization. It has not been possible, according to Gundel, op. cit. (on p. 47 n. 4 above), 40, to trace any lasting influence of Roman tactics on the early Germans' methods of warfare.

[3] Tacitus, *H* iv. 17 'nunc easdem omnium partis, addito si quid militaris disciplinae in castris Romanorum viguerit'.

(p. 82 f. below), the units of the two opposing armies were more highly organized and controlled than they had been a few years earlier. The barbarians kept some of their forces in reserve, and the warriors obeyed the orders of their respective leaders. The battle was not fought by the various retinues and kinship-groups acting as independent units: the whole levy on either side seemed to have been organized under a central command.[1] Tacitus believed that they had acquired this advanced military technique as a result of long years of campaigning against the Imperial forces; and it cannot be doubted that this is part of the explanation. But many other Germanic peoples fought frequently against the Romans without altering their old methods of making war. Why then did the followers of Arminius and Maroboduus do so? We may suggest that they were able to practise Roman methods of warfare because their social organization in general was in a more advanced state of change than that of many other Germans: the warriors were no longer all upon the one footing, and the chiefs were no longer merely the first among equals. Indeed, Maroboduus had already suppressed the old institutions of government among the Marcomanni and had replaced them by a personal tyranny. And only a few years were to pass before Arminius believed that he could do the same among the Cherusci; and although his belief turned out to have been unfounded, he cannot have been altogether without grounds for holding it. The adoption of something like a State army was only possible when something like a State organization of society in general had taken the place of the organization based on the clans.[2] More-

[1] Id., *A* ii. 45. 3; Velleius, ii. 109. 1.
[2] But note these peoples' low stage of cultural development as compared with that of the Pannonians who joined in the revolt against the

over, at the time when Tacitus wrote the *Germania* the Chatti, too, had developed this more advanced type of disciplined army. But it is hardly a coincidence that their warriors were unusually well equipped with metal tools, that more abundant food supplies were available to their levies than to those of other Germanic peoples, and that a greater number of the Chatti were entirely divorced from the work of production than was customary elsewhere in Germany.[1] For some reason their economic development was exceptionally high, and as a result the old form of society would soon be a thing of the past among them. And the general social change had brought about a change in the nature of their military organization, their methods of warfare, and their weapons.[2]

This alteration in the character of the army, which presupposes a higher degree of coercive power than existed elsewhere in Germany, is known to have affected three peoples, the Marcomanni, the Cherusci, and the Chatti; and there is no reason to think that any of the others had yet taken this step. But among one of these three peoples the final stage had already been reached.

As early as the reign of Augustus came the first instance, so far as is recorded, of the complete overthrow of the old social system and its replacement by something more autocratic. Maroboduus, leader of the Marcomanni, was the first German known to us who transformed his position from that of a confederate chieftain dependent on the goodwill of his people into

Romans in A.D. 6: Velleius, ii. 110. 5 'in omnibus autem Pannoniis non disciplinae tantummodo sed linguae quoque notitia Romanae, plerisque etiam litterarum usus et familiaris animorum erat exercitatio'.

[1] Tacitus, *G* xxx. 2–3, xxxi. 4 f.

[2] This type of change was viewed with concern by the Romans: Seneca, *de Ira* i. 11. 4.

that of a monarch who could impose his will on his subjects. In one of the last years B.C. Maroboduus had withdrawn the Marcomanni in the face of the Roman advance into western Germany and had led them from the Main valley to new homes in Bohemia. Before making the move he had succeeded—though perhaps not without meeting some resistance—in establishing himself as a permanent autocrat not subject to the people's control but certainly the object of their hatred. In Bohemia he built himself a 'palace' which lay close to, but was nevertheless distinct from, his people's stronghold.[1] The distinction between his former position as the elected military leader of the Marcomanni and his new position as their ruler was observed and clearly defined by a contemporary Roman author, who had himself served on the German frontier.[2] In his new position he had extended his power over several other Germanic peoples. Indeed, his empire was very large, for from his headquarters in Bohemia he even ruled over the Lombards, who are thought to have lived at this date in the lower part of the basin of the Elbe, northeast of Hanover. But we do not know precisely how he won his despotic power or what role his retinue played in winning it for him. It is scarcely a coincidence, however, that the first Germanic autocrat made his appearance in exactly that part of the Germanic

[1] Tacitus, A ii. 62. 3; cf. Strabo, vii. 1. 3. I suspect that Tacitus has Maroboduus' kingdom particularly in mind when he mentions the powerful position of freedmen in 'iis gentibus quae regnantur', G xxv. 3.

[2] Velleius, ii. 108. 2; cf. Tacitus, A ii. 44. 3 'Maroboduum regis nomen invisum apud populares . . . habebat'. From *Monumentum Ancyranum*, xxxii 'ad me supplices confugerunt reges . . . Sugambrorum Maelo, Marcomanorum Sueborum . . .] rus' (cf. Suetonius, *Aug.* xxi. 1), it would seem that some Marcomanni, including one of their leading men, went over to the Romans sooner than submit to Maroboduus, though Augustus may be referring to some otherwise unknown event which took place in 10–9 B.C. or somewhat earlier.

world where Roman influence was most intense, where the private ownership of property was most highly developed, and where a colony of Roman traders was continuously engaged in commerce and in lending money to the native population (p. 22 above). Tacitus has already suggested to us that when privately owned wealth accumulates in a primitive society, power—and he means coercive power—tends to become concentrated in one central authority (p. 10 above).

It is not accidental, then, that Maroboduus' name is also associated with another innovation in Germanic history. In general, the wars fought between themselves by the Germanic peoples in the days of Caesar and Tacitus and indeed for long after were fought for the possession of disputed lands, for cattle, prestige, and so on.[1] In extreme cases they might end in the migration of the weaker side to territories of greater security, or in the exhaustion of the contending parties, or even in something like the annihilation of one of the peoples concerned.[2] But from the beginning of the Christian era a new kind of war begins to make its appearance, though for many centuries it remained a rare phenomenon. This is the war which ends in the subjugation of the beaten side and in its reduction to the status of subjects of the conquerors. When Procopius noted a war of this kind among the Germans of the sixth century, he turned

[1] It would be interesting to know how much of the restlessness and raiding in the first century A.D. was due to the dislocation of their economy brought about by the transition from matrilineal to patrilineal inheritance of property: see Miss Phillpotts, op. cit. (on p. 17 n. 1 above), 270 n. 1.

[2] For such wars see e.g. Caesar, *BG* i. 31. 10 (cf. 14), iv. 1. 1 f.; Tacitus, *G* xxxiii; cf. *A* xiii. 56. 6; Dio Cassius, liv. 36. 3; Jordanes, *Get.* xvii. 97 f.; Procopius, *BG* vi. 14. 27; Bede, *HE* iv. 14 (16), etc.; and esp. Mela, iii. 3 'bella cum finitimis gerunt: causas eorum ex libidine arcessunt, neque imperitandi prolatandique quae possident (nam ne illa quidem enixe colunt) sed ut circa ipsos quae iacent vasta sint'.

aside to comment on its rarity even at that date.[1]
Tacitus thought it a characteristic of the Germanic
peoples that they would not submit to paying tribute,[2]
and cases where they were obliged to do so by other
Germans cannot often have existed in his time, for there
was no administrative machinery for collecting tribute,
taxes, or the like.[3] But after Maroboduus had overthrown the old form of government among the Marcomanni and had moved his people into Bohemia, he
engaged in a series of wars with his new neighbours,
some of whom were Germanic, which left them subject
to his rule; and he forced their warriors to accompany
him on his campaigns and to fight for him.[4] And the
readiness with which two of his subject peoples turned
against him when he was attacked by an external power
suggests that his rule was felt to be in some degree
oppressive.[5] Again, at the end of the first century A.D. a
Celtic-speaking people called the Cotini were paying
quantities of iron to the Quadi, who were closely associated with the Marcomanni.[6] Now, the old tribal order
had no place for ruler and ruled; and it is significant
that the first instance of the subjugation of German by
German and the first example of a kingdom oppressively
exploited by a German monarch are found precisely at
the place (Bohemia) where the old social order first
broke down.

[1] Procopius, *BG* vi. 14. 9, though cf. Eugippius, *Vita S. Severini* xvii. 2.
xxxi. 1. The major exception on the Continent is the wars of Ermanaric:
Jordanes, *Get.* xxiii. 116 f.

[2] *G* xxix. 2, xliii. 1.

[3] But Vannius was able to collect *vectigalia* for 30 years: id., *A* xii. 29. 3.
It is not easy to believe in Ariovistus' *vectigalia* and *stipendium* mentioned
in Caesar, *BG* i. 36. 4 f., unless he used Celtic machinery to collect them.

[4] Tacitus, *A* ii. 45. 1. For a parallel cf. the treatment of the Burgundians
by the Franks after 534, according to Procopius, *BG* v. 13. 3, though see
also vi. 12. 38.

[5] Tacitus, loc. cit.          [6] Id., *G* xliii. 2.

We have seen above how the tribal nobility was in process of withdrawing itself from productive work towards the end of the first century A.D. and how it had taken the first steps towards establishing itself as a political force uncontrolled by the mass of the warriors. We now see that in communities where the State can hardly be said to have existed the nobility had created for itself some of the organs of State, though in an embryonic form. The administration of justice was being taken out of the hands of the kindreds, and legal decisions were on the way to being forcibly imposed by the leading men. Not only were the free warriors being depressed into the position of soldiers obedient to their officers' commands, but the possibility of holding entire peoples in subjection had already been realized for a while in Bohemia. The Germanic State cannot be said to have come wholly into existence until the Visigoths and the Burgundians had settled in Gaul in the fifth century; but it was not born fully grown and without antecedents from the heads of Wallia and Gundahar.

# CHAPTER THREE

# ROMAN DIPLOMACY
# AND THE GERMANS

MORE is known about the history of the Cherusci than about that of any other Germanic people in this period, and a short summary of it, familiar though it may be, will provide concrete illustrations of some of the points under discussion. It will also introduce a factor to which we have only referred incidentally so far—the direct interference of the Roman government in the internal affairs of the Germanic peoples and the effect of this interference on the tribal institutions. After dealing with the Cherusci we shall turn to the fragmentary information which has survived—mostly in the *Annals* of Tacitus—relating to the Romans' treatment of the other peoples of Germany.

## *1. The Cherusci*

The Cherusci, living on either side of the middle Weser and extending eastwards as far as the Elbe, were one of the peoples who chose their war-chieftains 'in accordance with their noble birth' (p. 34 above); that is to say, there was a 'royal stock' among them as among the Batavians and other peoples, and from the members of this 'royal stock' the chieftain had to be elected. In A.D. 6, then, the Cherusci chose as their military leader a young man aged 26 named Arminius, the son of Sigimer, one of their leading men. For some years (probably A.D. 4–6) Arminius had commanded a company of German auxiliaries in the Roman army with such distinction that the Romans had given him their citizen-ship, the rank of knight, and perhaps even the name Arminius.[1] But it was under his leadership in A.D. 9 that the Cherusci destroyed the three legions of Quintilius Varus and thus freed western Germany from direct Roman domination.

Now, not all the Cherusci regarded the expulsion of the Romans with unmixed delight. Arminius' father-in-law Segestes had also been presented with Roman citizenship by Augustus when the Romans still occupied Germany; and he proved himself to be a man of out-standing loyalty to the Imperial government.[2] From the very beginning he had been opposed to Arminius' plans for a revolt. On many occasions, and even at a feast held on the night before the fateful battle, he had gone so far as to betray the plans of the Cherusci to Varus,[3] and he afterwards boasted loudly of his treachery.[4] He is reported to have said in the year 15 that from the day when Augustus had given him the citizenship he had chosen his friends and enemies to suit the interests of the Romans because he wished for peace rather than for war with Rome and because he believed the interests of the Romans and the Germans to be identical.[5] Segestes had suffered no oppression under the Roman occupa-tion. The Romans had long experience in winning over the nobility of a newly conquered tribal people, in detaching them from the manner of life of their humbler followers, and in absorbing them into Roman ways. Their practice was to establish a loyal native ruling

[1] Velleius, ii. 118. 2; Tacitus, *A* ii. 10. 3.
[2] Ibid., i. 58. 2; cf. 55. 2.
[3] Ibid., i. 55. 3, 58. 3 f.; Strabo, vii. 1. 4; Velleius, ii. 118, 4; Florus, ii. 30. 33 (iv. 12. 33); cf. Dio Cassius, lvi. 19. 3.
[4] Tacitus, *A* i. 58. 1–5.
[5] Ibid.

class living in cities and having a substantial stake in the continuance of Roman rule. The native chiefs would learn to become Roman landowners receiving rents from the native peasants who had previously been their fellow-tribesmen. They would learn Latin, wear Roman dress, use Roman furniture in their houses, and might even marry Italians or others who settled in their country. These methods had been tried among the Germans east of the Rhine, and not without success.[1] The Romans merely developed the already existing distinction between the leading men and the common warriors. The fact was that in the old clan society there was no institution which could protect the social position of the new nobles against the communal traditions of the kindreds or against the ambitions of rivals: even the retinue was sometimes inadequate for this purpose. But under the Roman occupation precisely this supra-tribal authority was supplied. Under the strong rule of the Roman civilian and military officials a noble like Segestes could often ensure his social position among his people, a position which was now enhanced by his Roman manners and his veneer of Roman civilization and by the confidence which the Romans might show in him. If the Roman peace were imposed upon Germany there could be few threats to his position or his wealth from rival members of the local nobility; and the limits which the clan system set to his wealth, influence, and power would quickly die away. We need not doubt the sincerity of the plea which Tacitus ascribes to Segestes: he had not sided with the Romans through hatred of his people or in the hope of securing some specific reward from the enemy.[2] He simply wished to dissociate himself from any act of 'treachery' to the Imperial power which

---

[1] Dio Cassius, lvi. 18. 2–4.    [2] Tacitus, A i. 58. 2, 6.

he admired and from whose presence in Germany he had profited. Moreover, he even saw himself in A.D. 15 in the role of one who would reconcile the Germans to the Romans if his people should repent of their destruction of Varus' army. As Tacitus depicts him, he seems almost to have been toying in A.D. 15, when Germanicus' armies were operating in Germany, with the idea of a restoration of Roman power east of the Rhine.[1] In A.D. 9 he had been compelled by the only coercive power that existed among the Cherusci, that is, by public opinion, to take part, however reluctantly, in the struggle for freedom;[2] and although many of his kindred and 'companions' were given booty from the spoils taken from the army of Varus, Segestes himself had only engaged in the battle against his will.[3] Accordingly, he left his people in A.D. 15 after events which will be examined later (p. 79 f. below), and with his kindred and retinue lived in security west of the Rhine when the Roman armies were gathering their strength for a new campaign of devastation among the people whom he had abandoned. And after the campaigns of Germanicus were over, while himself treated with respect by the Romans, he watched some of his closest kin being dragged along in the triumphal procession of Germanicus at Rome on 26 May, A.D. 17.[4]

Now, Segestes was not an isolated phenomenon among the leading men of the Cherusci. It is true that the bulk of the German optimates, including those of the Cherusci, longed as their followers did for the old days of freedom which they had enjoyed before the Romans came;[5] for, among much else, if the establish-

---

[1] Ibid.  [2] Ibid., 55. 4.  [3] Ibid., 57. 6.
[4] Strabo, vii. 4. 1.
[5] Dio Cassius, lvi. 18. 4 (who exaggerates); Tacitus, A ii. 15; et al.

ment of Roman power among them might secure the social position of some, it might equally well thwart the ambitions of others.[1] And besides, they had good reason to remember the greed, cruelty, and truculence of the Roman occupiers.[2] Yet the process which led a section of the nobles to show Roman sympathies had made no little progress in Arminius' day and was not simply in its earliest stages. The Imperial occupation of Germany, short-lived though it was, had not been in vain. For while the case of Segestes was extreme, it was no more so than that of Arminius' own brother Flavus (as he was called by the Romans). Even after the victory over Varus[3] he had served with distinction and with outstanding 'loyalty' (as the Romans called it) as a mounted scout in the Imperial forces[4] when Tiberius came down to the Rhine frontier early in A.D. 10; and he was still serving with them during Germanicus' campaign against his fellow-tribesmen six years later. In the opinion of the Cherusci no one fought against his countrymen and the gods of his fathers with more resolution than Flavus had done; and even after a generation had passed, his 'treachery' (as the Cherusci believed it to be) was still vividly remembered.[5] Moreover, there is reason to think that some of the Cherusci,

[1] Cf. the sentiments of certain Gauls in a somewhat similar situation in the winter of 58–57 B.C.: 'in Gallia a potentioribus atque eis qui ad conducendos homines facultates habebant vulgo regna occupabantur, qui minus facile eam rem imperio nostro consequi poterant', Caesar, *BG* ii. 1. 4.

[2] Tacitus, *A* ii. 15. 4. Note Varus' attitude towards those whom he governed: 'concepit esse homines qui nihil praeter vocem membraque haberent hominum', Velleius, ii. 117. 3.

[3] Tacitus, *A* ii. 9. 2.   [4] Ibid., xi. 16. 6; cf. ii. 10. 2.

[5] Ibid., ii. 9–10, xi. 16. 8. Flavus' son (ibid., xi. 16. 3) and his brother Arminius both had the Roman citizenship so that Flavus himself probably had it too. Segestes' brother Segimerus would also seem to have been faint-hearted in opposing the Romans, though Segimerus' son Sesithacus was more suspect: ibid., i. 71. 1 f.

who shrank from the extreme step of leaving their people outright and who had not gone off to serve with the Roman forces, felt much as Segestes had felt. These men were reluctant, it seems, to follow Arminius in resisting Germanicus' punitive expedition into Germany in A.D. 15; and the news that Segestes had surrendered to the Romans and had been kindly received by Germanicus filled them with hopes of reaching an accommodation with the Roman authorities.[1] Indeed, a tantalizing sentence in one of our sources of information tells us that in the first year of the Christian era some of the Cherusci had been expelled from among their people, and that L. Domitius Ahenobarbus, who wished to have them restored 'by others' of the Cherusci, failed in his attempt and brought them into some discredit.[2] It is unfortunate that we do not know the identity of these exiles, who do not appear to have been numerous. If they were merely a handful of rank-and-file warriors or even a faction of the nobles expelled because of some purely domestic quarrel, it is not altogether easy to understand why Ahenobarbus was so anxious to see them restored and why a Roman historian thought the matter worthy of mention in his brief narrative. It may be, then, that they were some of those nobles on whom Roman power in Germany largely rested and whose attitude to the Roman occupiers was little less friendly than that which Segestes was to show a few years later. If so, the tension between pro-Roman and anti-Roman forces among the Cherusci can be traced back to the middle of the period of the Roman occupation; and it is noteworthy that the opponents of the pro-Roman faction were strong enough to expel them even at a time when the Romans were in nominal

[1] Ibid., 59. 1.      [2] Dio Cassius, lv. 10a. 3.

occupation of their country. But it is even more note-worthy that such a pro-Roman faction existed at all and that it by no means disappeared after Varus' defeat.

Moreover, pro-Roman leanings were not confined to a section of the Cheruscan nobility. In A.D. 9 during the rising against the Romans Arminius had to throw into chains a chief of the Ampsivarii named Boiocalus, who thereafter went on to fight in the Roman army under Tiberius and Germanicus, to serve the Romans for 50 years, and to contrive to keep his people subject to them throughout that time.[1] There can be little doubt that in and after A.D. 9 many an optimate among the Germans regretted, perhaps as keenly as Segestes, the expulsion of the Romans; and in the revolt of A.D. 69 such men were sometimes more willing than the common warriors to come to terms with the enemy.[2] It is true that in many ways the conquest of Germany had been superficial and that the conquerors had not been able to set up direct rule over all the peoples who nominally submitted to them: the elections to the chieftainships no doubt continued to be held in the years immediately before A.D. 9. But if the Romans were not in a position to abolish the popular elections they could certainly influence them and secure the election of comparatively 'loyal' chiefs. They had ways and means of ensuring the appointment of the right men to high office even among nominally independent peoples, as the Celt Dumnorix had reason to know in Julius Caesar's day.[3] If men of the stamp of

---

[1] Tacitus, *A* xiii. 55. 2. In 17 B.C. (*Cambridge Ancient History*, x, 360) the Sugambri, Usipetes, and Tencteri decided to attack Roman Gaul, and their first action was to catch *and crucify* some of their own number (Dio Cassius, liv. 20. 4 f.) Why?

[2] Tacitus, *H* iv. 56, 70, v. 25.

[3] Caesar, *BG* i. 18. 8. What were the precise mechanics by which Caesar so often achieved this result? See *BG* v. 4. 2 f., 25. 2 f., 54. 2, vi. 8. 8, *et al.*, all referring to nominally independent peoples.

Boiocalus and Segestes were chosen as chiefs of the various peoples in the period of the Roman occupation it is not difficult to understand why Germany made no move to free herself in A.D. 6, 7, and 8, when the resources of the Romans were stretched to their very limits by the great rebellion of Illyricum: it was not easy for the tribesmen to move against the will of the chiefs and leading men and without their initiative.[1] Before they could take their fortunes into their hands they had to wait until the Romans unsuspectingly permitted, or perhaps even encouraged, the election of one who no doubt seemed utterly loyal to them, the Roman soldier, citizen, and knight Arminius.

After their liberation from the Romans in A.D. 9 the Cheruscan warriors had still to face these facts. When the Romans withdrew to the Rhine in consequence of the disaster to Varus' legions they had hopes that the Cherusci were beginning to split into two hostile factions grouped around Arminius and Segestes;[2] and indeed violent quarrels broke out between the two with fluctuating results.[3] At length in A.D. 15 Arminius, supported by the mass of the Cherusci, laid siege to Segestes. The latter had isolated himself from the people and was supported only by his kindred and his retinue, who however amounted to a strong force. Arminius had correctly interpreted the feelings of the Cherusci as a whole when he urged them to resist the punitive raid launched by Germanicus across the Rhine in that year. Segestes, on the other hand, would appear to have advised them to remain neutral when

---

[1] Tacitus, A i. 55. 3, cf. the position among the Iazyges, id., H iii. 5.

[2] Id., A i. 55. 2. Arminius' marriage to Segestes' daughter Thusnelda intensified but did not create the enmity between the two men: ibid., 4 auctis.

[3] Ibid., 58. 5.

neighbouring peoples were attacked by the Imperial armies, or at any rate he did not show much enthusiasm for the warlike plans of Arminius. During the siege he appealed for help against his own people to Germanicus who was now operating in Germany and was in fact on his way home after devastating the lands of the Chatti. Germanicus welcomed the opportunity. He attacked the besiegers, rescued Segestes and the throng of his kindred and retinue, and allowed them to live inside the Roman frontier.[1] And there Segestes told him how he preferred the old conditions of Roman occupation to the new ways of freedom, peace to disturbance, Roman rule to tribal conflict;[2] but he did not mention that to the bulk of his people Roman rule meant 'slavery'.[3] Tacitus is not far off the mark when he represents Arminius as saying that the Germans should show no less resolution in expelling such a 'satellite of Caesar' from Germany than they had shown in killing Quintilius Varus.[4]

This was a struggle, then, between the people under their elected chief and a member of the nobility supported by his kindred and retinue in alliance with the Romans. The point of view of the two contending parties can be understood. Segestes had been opposed to the attack on Varus' army. He and others like him saw that it was in their interest to live under direct Roman rule in Germany if possible; but, if that was not possible, then as a last resort to leave Germany altogether and live in the Imperial provinces.[5] On the other hand,

[1] Ibid., i. 57, 71. 1–2.
[2] Ibid., 58. 6.
[3] Ibid., ii. 15. 4; cf. *H* iv. 14, 17. Tacitus himself uses the word of Roman rule in *A* ii. 73. 3; cf. xiv. 31. 4, *Agric.* xiv. 2.
[4] *A* ii. 45. 4, referring to Maroboduus in A.D. 17.
[5] But Roman rule did not always succeed in maintaining the position of the nobles if Dio Cassius, lv. 10a. 3, is to be interpreted as suggested on p. 77 above.

the mass of the tribesmen tended not without reason to
be unremittingly hostile to the Romans, to the punish-
ments inflicted by Roman law, to the relentless collec-
tion of the taxes, and in general to 'the rods and axes' of
the lictors.[1] They would recognize that while their
elected leader would defend their independence and
their fame, the pro-Roman noble would lead them only
to 'slavery'.[2] When Arminius spoke of Segestes and also
of his own brother Flavus, who was serving in the
Roman army, as 'traitors' to their kindred and their
people he hardly exaggerated.[3] It was in part through
such men as Segestes[4] that the Romans had exercised
their authority in Germany during their occupation of
it; and accordingly it was a matter of no great difficulty
for Arminius to whip up strong resentment among the
tribesmen against such of the nobility as showed sym-
pathy for the Romans, took refuge among them, or
accepted their priesthoods and their money: it was
through such men that direct Roman rule might one
day be restored east of the Rhine (for, whatever official
Roman policy may have been, Tacitus is no doubt
correct in representing the Germans as expecting
in A.D. 15–16 and later that the Romans would try
to re-establish their rule in Germany). Many years
after the defeat of Varus the cry that Roman power
was being restored in Germany could still bring
into existence something of a feeling of solidarity,
something of a willingness to act in co-operation

[1] Tacitus, *A* i. 59. 6 f. (cf. Caratacus in xii. 34. 3), *H* iv. 32.
[2] Id., *A* i. 59. 8.
[3] Ibid., ii. 10. 1, xi. 16. 8. It would be interesting to have more information about the social status of the deserters mentioned in i. 56. 5
(Chatti), ii. 12. 1 (Cherusci), *H* v. 18 (Batavi).
[4] And also 'Inguiomerus Arminii patruus, vetere apud Romanos
auctoritate', id., *A* i. 60. 1, though there is no indication that Inguiomerus
was reluctant to join in the revolt of A.D. 9.

with one another, among the different Germanic peoples.[1]

Moreover, it was not only to the Romans that a noble and his retinue might desert. In A.D. 17 Arminius was the champion of tribal liberties among other peoples besides the Cherusci, for Germanic leaders often interfered in the internal affairs of neighbouring peoples so as to overthrow a chieftain whose pro-Roman leanings were too pronounced, or who had established himself as a despot, or the like.[2] After Maroboduus had made himself autocrat among the Marcomanni and had subjugated some of the neighbouring peoples, he stood aside and did nothing during the great events of A.D. 9, and hence he was regarded by Arminius as a mere satellite of the Emperor and as a traitor to the Germanic peoples.[3] Arminius championed those oppressed by Maroboduus, both native Marcomanni and foreign subjects; but as soon as he went to war with him in A.D. 17 the Cherusci learned the lengths to which the jealousies of their leading men, even men of the same clan, could go. Arminius' paternal uncle Inguiomerus had had high influence with the Romans during the occupation, but unlike Segestes had resolutely opposed Germanicus in A.D. 15 and 16.[4] As soon as the war against Maroboduus opened, however, he refused to obey any longer his brother's son, who was younger than he by many years. Accordingly, he deserted to the tyrant with such a large retinue that he made the two conflicting sides more nearly equal in strength, whereas

[1] Ibid., i. 59, ii. 45. 4; cf. 10. 1 *opes Caesaris*, xi. 16. 5.
[2] Ibid., ii. 44. 3, 62. 2 f., 88. 1, xi. 16. 5, 17. 5 (Italicus *restored* by Lombard aid), xii. 29. 2; Dio Cassius, lxvii. 5. 1. Such interference was not always due to high-minded motives: Tacitus, *A* xii. 29. 3.
[3] Ibid., ii. 45. 4.
[4] Ibid., i. 60. 1, 68, ii. 17. 8, 21. 2.

before his desertion the Cherusci had had a considerable superiority.[1]

In the cases of Segestes and Inguiomerus, then, the retinue fought for its leader, but the victory which the leader fought for was not the victory of his people but of his people's enemies (p. 31 above). This was the first of two truths which the Cherusci saw demonstrated in the years following A.D. 9: the community of interests between a leading man together with his retinue and a hostile, external, tyrannical power, whether Roman or Germanic, might well be stronger than the ties which bound him to his own people. Some, though by no means all, of the leading men felt that their real interests lay with those who would suppress the old liberties. The second truth which the Cherusci had now to learn was that even the most renowned chieftain, the strongest opponent of tyrannical ideas and practices in others, might himself one day undertake to destroy the popular liberties which he had spent his life in defending.

In A.D. 19, after serving the Cherusci loyally for twelve years on end as their elected military leader, Arminius, 'beyond doubt the liberator of Germany' (as Tacitus calls him), began himself to aim at destroying the freedom of the clans and at establishing a personal despotism over the Cherusci, just as he had seen his enemy Maroboduus do among the Marcomanni. And as he himself had interfered in Marcomannic affairs to overthrow Maroboduus, so a leading man of the Chatti, whose name is given as Adgandestrius, is said to have considered a plan to poison Arminius, though the plan came to nothing.[2] But Arminius underestimated the strength of his countrymen's independent spirit. Supported no doubt by his retinue he fought against his

[1] Ibid., ii. 45. 2.          [2] Ibid., ii. 88. 1, 3.

people without decisive result: he had followed in the footsteps of Segestes after all. In the end he was killed by treachery by his own kinsmen.[1] Now, of all crimes known to a clan society none is regarded with more horror than the murder of kinsman by kinsman; and although no details are available about the assassination of Arminius the fact that the deed was actually done by his kindred is a striking indication of the intensity of the feelings aroused by his anti-tribal activities. The last stage of Arminius' career shows that, given the direction in which Germanic society was moving at that time, even the most heroic of war-leaders and the staunchest champion of the old freedom, a man who had spent his life in uncompromising warfare against external and internal enemies of freedom, might sooner or later be tempted to overthrow the social system which he had hitherto supported.

The subsequent history of the Cherusci, in so far as we know it, is illuminating. Soon after the defeat of Varus in A.D. 9 the Roman government had hoped—and not without reason—that internal struggles would cripple the strength of the Cherusci (p. 79 above). When Germanicus was recalled from the Rhine frontier in A.D. 16 the government still believed that his work against the Germans would be completed by 'internal dissensions', a phrase by which our authority does not mean struggles carried on by one people against another but rather the struggles which, it was hoped, would break out inside each of the peoples in question.[2] When the Cherusci reappear in history in A.D. 47 the Roman government's judgement had been proved correct. In the interval since Arminius' day the Cherusci had been racked by civil war, and all their leading men including

[1] Ibid. *propinquorum*.　　　[2] Ibid., ii. 26. 3.

the whole of their 'royal stock' had been wiped out with the exception of Italicus alone, the son of Arminius' renegade brother Flavus (p. 76 above); and this Italicus was now living at Rome, where indeed he had been born.[1] The cause of this slaughter has not been recorded; but in view of the course which Cheruscan history had taken in the previous generation it may seem that one or other of two alternative explanations is likely to be correct. It may be that the nobility as a whole had been trying to overthrow the old system of government in which the final decision in all matters of importance had lain with the assembly of the warriors, and in making this attempt had tried to reach an accommodation with the Romans which would secure them in a new position where the assembly could no longer restrict their powers. If this is so, we may think that the nobility had been wiped out by the common warriors because of their co-operation with the Romans. On the other hand, it appears improbable that the nobility would have been unanimous on this issue; and a more likely explanation perhaps is that the nobility was divided, for in Arminius' day only a minority, and perhaps a small minority, of the nobles had shown pro-Roman leanings. In this case we must suppose that some of the optimates had continued the policy which Arminius had pursued in his great days but that others had shared the attitude of Segestes. If so, it would seem that the struggles which had broken out among the nobles themselves on this issue had resulted in their mutual destruction.

However that may be, Italicus alone was left alive: and when the Emperor Claudius restored him to the Cherusci to be their chief, the returned exile was

---

[1] Ibid., xi. 16. 1.

welcome enough at first, since he had taken no part in
the recent strife. But a number of the tribesmen soon
began to grow suspicious of the power which he was
gathering into his hands, of the increase of Roman
influence, and of the Roman manners of their new
leader. They and neighbouring peoples, too, began to
think that Roman power was being restored in Germany through him. And indeed before Italicus had left
Rome the Emperor had impressed on him that he was
going to the Cherusci not as a tribal leader to give
guidance to his followers but as a Roman citizen to rule
a foreign people.[1] Claudius, it would seem, did not propose that Italicus should be content with the old conception of a chieftain's position as being based on
personal influence and prestige. His intention was that
Italicus should not *lead* but should *govern* his people and
that he should do so according to Roman ideas of
power, coercion, and government. Hence, Italicus'
opponents gathered a powerful force which included a
number of foreign warriors. But the bulk of the Cherusci
still supported Italicus—the rank and file would no
doubt be slow to desert the man who according to
custom was their rightful leader;[2] and so in the upshot
Italicus defeated his enemies. But then the warriors
learned the mistake which they had made, for having
rid himself of his sharpest critics Italicus became oppressive to many of the rest of the people, and so was
driven out. The forces which still supported him in

[1] Ibid., 3. It would be interesting to know how the Suebic king mentioned in *H* iii. 5 and 21 *fin.* had also acquired the name Italicus. It is
probably no coincidence that the Romans could rely on the loyalty of the
Suebi when this Italicus was their leader.

[2] Id., *A* xi. 17. 1, shows that most of the Cherusci supported Italicus
since some of the opposing forces were foreigners; and § 5 *vulgus* suggests
that the rank and file was fairly solid for him. The opposition may have
consisted of some of the retinue-leaders.

Cheruscan society were now too weak to restore him unaided; and hence he was eventually restored only by the arms of the Lombards, the north-eastern neighbours of his people.[1]

No more is heard of the Cherusci until about the year 85 when Domitian was Emperor. Their leader now was one Chariomerus, whose relationship to Italicus and the 'royal stock' is unknown. He continued the tradition of Italicus as Italicus had continued that of Segestes and Flavus. Chariomerus displayed such a friendship for the Romans that the Chatti, the hereditary enemies of his people, attacked him as Arminius for the same reason had once attacked Maroboduus, and drove him and his retinue to take refuge with his friends the Romans. Evidently the pro-Roman sympathies of at least some sections of the Cheruscan nobility were as strong towards the end of the century as they had been at its beginning. Indeed, while Segestes and those who thought as he did were a minority of the nobles, it is not certain that the pro-Roman element among the aristocracy was so small a minority in the days of Italicus and Chariomerus. At any rate, Segestes and (in his last phase) Arminius seem to have been easier than Italicus and Chariomerus to isolate and destroy.

Although our abbreviated authority says nothing of the opposition from among the people to this pro-Roman tendency, there is no reason to doubt that the mass of the Cherusci were as independent-minded now as they had been in the time of Arminius and that they were not wholly unwilling to see the Chatti interfere in their affairs; for although one of our last glimpses of Chariomerus shows him effecting his return to his people, yet he was eventually abandoned even by his

[1] Ibid.

retinue when he gave hostages to Rome. He was expelled again, and he received money but no military aid from Domitian.[1] There followed a lengthy period of peace and exhaustion in which, we may be sure, the retinues of the leading men melted away, and the young warriors of the Cheruscan nobility, in so far as they had survived, went to find booty and renown in the retinues of foreign peoples.[2] At the end of the century the people of Arminius, the destroyers of Quintilius Varus, were of negligible importance beside the Chauci and the Chatti.[3] Their continual struggles with the Chatti, who lived to the south-west around the upper Weser and the Diemel, helped to weaken the Cherusci; but the issue which divided and destroyed them was the question of their relations with the Romans. We have suggested that that question was itself merely the central point in a wider problem. Some members of the native nobility did not support Rome for purely idealistic reasons: they did so because they saw in the extension of Roman power some guarantee for the new social position which they were trying to win in their own communities. Support for Rome was simply the focal point in the developing struggle between the leading men (or some of them) and the common warriors at home; and it was this struggle among the Cherusci which ended towards the close of the first century A.D. in the common ruin of the two contending parties.[4]

## 2. *Other Peoples*

As a result of the accumulation of privately owned

[1] Dio Cassius, lxvii. 5. 1.    [2] Tacitus, *G* xxxvi.
[3] Id., *A* xii. 28. 2, *G* xxxvi. 2.
[4] I take it that Claudian, *BG* 420, *iv cons. Hon.* 452 (and perhaps also *Paneg. Lat.* iv (x). 18. 1) are purely literary references and cannot be used to show that the Cherusci were still a threat or even that they existed in the fourth century.

wealth in the first century A.D. severe tensions began to pull Germanic society apart. We have now seen in addition something of the attraction of Rome for the Germanic optimates, and we have guessed at the reasons why Rome made so strong an appeal to some of them. In any case, there could be found both before and after A.D. 9 individual members of the native nobility and even groups of nobles who had favoured the Romans during the Roman occupation, who regretted their departure after Varus' defeat, and who were willing to side with them against the rank and file of their own countrymen. True, the development of pro-Roman sentiments was still in an early stage when Tacitus was writing in comparison with what was to be seen later. We do not yet hear of that open affability which in the fourth century might lead a German chieftain to cross the Imperial frontier merely in order to dine with the Roman officers on the other side.[1] We do not yet hear of such a desertion of the optimates to the Romans as we can trace among the Visigoths during the reign of Theodosius I. On the other hand, among the common warriors there may occasionally have been found individual traitors in the first century A.D. (p. 81 n. 3 above); but generally speaking the attitude of the tribesmen at large was as hostile to Rome as that of Arminius had been when he fought the armies of Varus and Germanicus.

Now, the existence of open or concealed pro-Roman sentiments in a section of the nobility among the frontier peoples was a temptation to the Imperial government to try to split the peoples in question, to separate the leaders from the rank and file, and so to destroy from the inside the peoples' power to damage Roman

---

[1] Amm. Marc. xxi. 4. 3, xxix. 6. 5; cf. xxxi. 5. 5.

interests. In fact, we rarely hear of difficulties or struggles in a border people without also hearing that the Romans—not always without an invitation to intervene[1]—took some direct or indirect part in fomenting or inflaming them. It might be argued, of course, that such struggles would only be reported by our authorities when the Imperial government was involved in them. But this is not quite the case, for Tacitus records a war of the Chatti and the Hermunduri with which the Romans do not seem to have concerned themselves.[2] That, however, was a war of people against people, whereas we are dealing with internal struggles inside the one people. The Imperial authorities were well aware of the tensions which existed in German society and indeed our knowledge of them is derived almost exclusively from the writings of a Roman senator.

We are not concerned here with the various devices employed by the Romans from time to time to prevent local raids on the provinces—the obligation to leave several miles of land immediately beyond the frontier uninhabited and uncultivated, the ban on the use of boats on the Danube and on setting foot on the islands in that river,[3] the limitation of trade to specific points on the frontier, the ban on crossing the Rhine at night or when carrying arms or when unescorted by Roman troops or without paying the toll.[4] Nor can we deal here with such crude devices as the assassination or kidnap-

[1] Dio Cassius, lxvii. 5. 2.

[2] Tacitus, *A* xiii. 57. 1–3.

[3] Dio Cassius, lxxi. 15–16, 19. 2 (Danube), lxxii. 3. 2; cf. Tacitus, *A* xiii. 54. 2; Amm. Marc. xvii. 13. 2 f. and 23, xix. 11. 1.

[4] Tacitus, *H* iv. 64 f., *G* xli. 1 f. For the restrictions imposed on trade across the frontier by the Romans see E. A. Thompson, *Hermes*, lxxxiv (1956), 376 n. 5. For a new case where the Romans enlisted into their army the warriors of three Germanic peoples whom they had recently defeated—presumably with the aim of weakening those peoples still further—see Pflaum, art. cit. (on p. 54 n. 2 above), 147.

ping of Germanic military leaders, a practice which usually ended by causing more damage to the Romans themselves than to those whose leaders they removed.[1] We are not concerned here with the nakedly aggressive wars which the Romans fought against various Germanic peoples, wars in which the indiscriminate burning and butchery carried out by the Roman armies might be described with complacency and satisfaction even by a comparatively humane Roman like Tacitus.[2] But in fact, although the Romans, if they got the opportunity to do so, would act as arbitrators in disputes between one barbarian people and another[3] or would intrigue so as to cause one barbarian people to go to war with another,[4] yet armed intervention by them in a war of barbarian against barbarian beyond the frontier was exceedingly rare;[5] it was the government's intention, if it could not disrupt the various peoples from the inside,

---

[1] Tacitus, *A* xi. 19. 3 f. (where Tacitus argues that two wrongs make a right, and represents Corbulo's critics as asserting that that is wrong which is inexpedient); Dio Cassius, lxxi. 14. 1; Amm. Marc. xxi. 4. 1 ff., xxix. 6. 5 (cf. Zosimus, iv. 16. 4), xxx. 5. 3, 7. 7 and 11; cf. A. Hirtius, *BG* viii. 23. 4, etc. But we hear of no reaction on the part of the Quadi when Caracalla killed their chief Gaiobomarus *c.* 215: Dio Cassius, lxxvii. 20. 3.

[2] Tacitus, *A* i. 51. 1 f., 56. 3, ii. 21. 3, *G* xxxiii. It would be easy to cite equally shocking passages in authors both earlier and later than Tacitus. An unusual type of tactic is recorded by Frontinus, *Strat.* ii. 11. 7: in A.D. 83 Domitian 'cum in finibus Cubiorum castella poneret, pro fructibus locorum, quae vallo comprehendebat, pretium solvi iussit; atque ita iustitiae fama omnium fidem adstrinxit'. To whom exactly did he pay the money?

[3] Dio Cassius, lxix. 9. 6; Eutropius, viii. 8; John of Antioch, frag. 115 *med.*; etc.

[4] e.g. Dio Cassius, lxxvii. 20. 3; Tacitus, *A* ii. 62. 1.

[5] It was presumably less rare in disturbed areas where the frontier was about to be pushed forward: ibid., xii. 40. 6; *Hermes*, art. cit. 374. This reluctance to interfere in civil wars across the frontier is another reason for doubting the accounts of the alleged civil war between Fritigern and Athanaric in which Valens is said to have intervened: see E. A. Thompson, *Journal of Ecclesiastical History*, vii (1956), 6 ff., but some examples are known from Justinian's reign: Procopius, *BG* vii. 34. 40, viii. 25. 14.

to allow them to destroy each other in wars of people against people[1] and simply to give diplomatic assistance to the weaker side. Thus, in A.D. 50, when the Suebi were in process of driving out their military leader Vannius, Claudius persistently refused to intervene in the civil war, though he promised Vannius a safe retreat in the Empire if his enemies should get the better of him. At the same time he moved a legion to a point on the Danube where its presence would lend moral support to the chief, who was the weaker of the combatants, and would at the same time prevent the stronger from crossing the frontier in pursuit of him.[2] At a later date (perhaps A.D. 98–9) Vestricius Spurinna managed to induce the Bructeri to accept against their will a military leader of his choice; and he won this success by means of a display of force though without actual fighting.[3] The procedure was not dissimilar to that which the Roman government adopted in the case of Chariomerus (p. 88 above). Our authority for what is known of Chariomerus' career makes it clear that when he asked Domitian for an alliance the Emperor refused it, though he did give him financial help. An exceptional case, though one which rather proves the rule, is also recorded from the reign of Domitian. The Lugii, who were at war with some of the Suebi asked the Emperor for a military alliance, as Chariomerus had done shortly before. This time Domitian did respond,

[1] Corbulo reached a satisfactory result on the eastern frontier in A.D. 60 when 'hostilem audaciam externo sanguine ultus est', Tacitus, *A* xiv. 23. 4; cf. *Agric.* xxxv. 2, *G* xxxiii. 2; Ambrose, *Ep.* xxiv. 8 (Migne, *PL* xvi. 1081 f.); Claudian, *vi cons. Hon.* 220 ff.; Orosius, vii. 43. 14; Malchus, frag. 15 (404. 1 ff., ed. Dindorf); cf. Zeno's use of Theodoric against Odoacer.

[2] Tacitus, *A* xii. 29. 2 f.

[3] Pliny, *Ep.* ii. 7. 2. On the date see Anderson, *Germania* 161 f.; R. Syme, *Journal of Roman Studies*, xxv (1935), 96.

but he sent the Lugii a force of only 100 horsemen who were intended to give prestige rather than positive military assistance to his allies. The sole result of sending them, so far as is known, was to infuriate the Suebi and induce them to prepare an attack across the Danube on the Roman provinces.[1]

The Imperial government, as we have said, were well aware that in many of their dealings with the northern barbarians it was not from the mass of the warriors but from the nobility that they might expect a degree of collaboration. They were also aware that if the leaders of a Germanic community were neutralized or won over it was difficult for the common warriors to initiate any major activity of their own: the assemblies could not function normally without the preliminary discussions of the leading men and without the proposals and initiative of the chiefs (p. 31 n. 2 above). The aim of Roman diplomacy, then—and it was based on long experience (see e.g. p. 78 n. 3 above)—was to keep in office or even to put into office[2] chieftains who would carry out a policy friendly to Rome, men on whose 'loyalty' the Imperial authorities could rely. And this they sometimes succeeded in doing, according to Tacitus, even in cases where their nominees were men who had so little support from their followers that 'their power and ascendency were derived from Roman authority' and from that alone. It is of great importance to note that sometimes the power with which the Romans could endow such a chief was coercive power of a kind which the ordinary Germanic leader did not enjoy: it was individual authority such as was essentially

[1] Dio Cassius, lxvii. 5. 2.
[2] At a later date when Roman power had declined this was regarded as a somewhat rare achievement: Aurelius Victor, *Caes.* 42. 21 f.

alien to early Germanic society.[1] Tacitus cites the Marcomanni and Quadi as examples, and he adds that it was unusual for the Imperial government to have to support them by force of arms: it was enough as a rule—though it had not been enough in the case of the Cheruscan Chariomerus—to support them with money, which gave them as much authority, he says, among their people as armed intervention would have done. We must draw a distinction here. It has been said of the chieftainship among many primitive societies of the modern world that 'no other feature of simple society suffers such rapid modification under the external influence of the European. . . . The European official who visits a new region will at once ask for the chief, by which he means a person with whom he can negotiate, and who will act as an intermediary between the people and himself. Sometimes the real chief steps forward, when he comes to wield powers of which till then he had not dreamed, so that the whole institution of chieftainship as well as the mode of government soon suffers great modification.'[2] Similar changes may well have

[1] Tacitus, *G* xlii. 2 *vis et potentia*, a wholly different phrase from anything that Tacitus uses elsewhere of the German chiefs' influence. The Romans' task among the Marcomanni may well have been facilitated by the fact that Maroboduus' tyranny had already dealt a blow at the old social system among them. Other examples of imposed chiefs (though perhaps not all had coercive power) are referred to in *A* xii. 29. 1; cf. ii. 63. 7; Pliny, loc. cit.; *SHA, Hadrian* xii. 7; Amm. Marc. xxix. 4. 7; Claudian, *In Eutrop.* i. 381; Libanius, *Or.* lix. 132 (A.D. 348–9), where Constans in 341–2 imposes pliable chiefs on the Franks; cf. Claudian, *i cons. Stil.* 236 ff. (It would be interesting to know how this was done, as the society of the Franks must have been very primitive at this date and the institution of the retinue cannot have been very highly developed.) H. Mattingly, *Coins of the Roman Empire in the British Museum*, iv (London, 1940), 204 no. 1274 (cf. 367 no. 2129), illustrates a coin of Antoninus Pius inscribed *rex quadis datus*, on which see E. Swoboda, *Carnuntum-Jahrbuch*, Beiheft 2 (1956), 5–12. Note also *SHA, Ant. Pius*, ix. 6. For the non-Germanic Sarmatians see Amm. Marc. xvii. 12. 20; Aur. Victor, loc. cit.

[2] W. H. R. Rivers, *Social Organization* (London, 1924), 165.

been brought about in some parts of Germany when the Romans arrived on the borders of the country: indeed, it is not easy to see how such changes could have been avoided. Is it likely, for instance, that Ariovistus' position was unaltered when the Roman government styled him 'Friend of the Roman People' in 59 B.C. and when Caesar tried to negotiate with him personally?[1] But such changes are not in themselves the result of deliberate policy. They are the unintended result of mere contact between two peoples at widely separated levels of development. What Tacitus has in mind, however, is something different. According to him, it was the deliberate policy of the Imperial government to endow with coercive, personal authority (*vis et potentia*) a chief who had not hitherto possessed it. Roman ideas of power were deliberately introduced into Germany.

The number of chiefs willing to co-operate with Rome was increased by the Imperial government's policy of taking the sons of leading men as hostages and of educating them at Rome and of bringing them up to feel themselves to be Romans and no longer Germans. When one of them was about to go back to his people the Emperor Claudius told him that he was going as a Roman citizen to govern a foreign people (p. 86 above). Such men on their return to Germany as chiefs would have new, Roman ideas of government and would be unlikely to submit without reluctance to the restraints which tribal society would try to impose on their influence. It may be no coincidence that the

[1] Caesar, *BG* i. 35. 2. Throughout his narrative of the campaign against Ariovistus Caesar seems to speak of him as a prince with personal power to make decisions (though note *BG* i. 43. 3) and he perhaps carried on many of his negotiations with him as though he were such. But in this part of his work Caesar is not concerned with anthropological niceties, and there is no reason to think that Ariovistus had any authority of a kind unknown elsewhere in Germany at that time.

earliest known example of the overthrow of the traditional social system was carried out by Maroboduus when he returned from a period spent in Rome as a hostage, where he had been well treated by Augustus.[1] These returned hostages, apart from having acquired Roman manners, would also be 'infected' with 'servility' towards the Roman government and could not fail to have learned something of the Roman technique of government.[2] Of all this Italicus the Cheruscan is a striking example. But sometimes if a suitable native candidate were not forthcoming the Romans would even manage to impose a foreigner upon a Germanic people to be their chief, and indeed the various peoples were not always averse to putting themselves voluntarily under the leadership of a foreigner.[3] The way for this was prepared by the custom of the young nobles who often served in the retinues of foreign chiefs and by the growing similarity of manners among the nobility of the various peoples (p. 58 above).

But how did Roman influence enable a chief, whom they found reliable, to maintain himself in power if in

---

[1] Strabo, vii. 1. 3. The policy of taking hostages was, of course, a flexible one and was not always applied: Dessau 986.

[2] Tacitus, *A* xi. 16. 7 *infectum servitio*; cf. ii. 2. 3 ff., xiv. 26. 1, xv. 1. 2. Note also xii. 10. 4 'principem patresque, quorum moribus adsuefactus (sc. the hostage) rex melior adsciceretur'.

[3] Tacitus, *G* xlii. 2; cf. *A* ii. 63. 7, xi. 18. 1. The Cherusci did not reject Italicus because his mother was the daughter of a Chattan chief, xi. 16. 2. The Burgundian king Gundioc was descended 'ex genere Athanarici', i.e. was of Visigothic descent: Greg. Tur. *HF* ii. 28. The Visigoth Aioulfus hoped to become king of the Suevi in Gallaecia in 457; Hydatius 187 (*Chronica Minora*, ii, 30). In 539–40 the Ostrogoths offered to make Belisarius their king, or rather Western Emperor, with themselves as his subjects: Procopius, *BG* vi. 29. 18 and 26, 30. 26. We hear ibid., vii. 2. 4 and 10, that Eraric, a Rugian, was made king of the Ostrogoths who objected to him not simply because he was a Rugian but because they thought that he was inadequate for the war against the Romans. In 553 the Ostrogoths offered to make the Alamannic Butilinus their king: Agathias, *Hist.* ii. 2. See also ibid., ii. 13, and Jordanes, *Get.* xxxiii. 174 f.

fact he did not have the confidence of his people—if indeed the people at large were so hostile to him that Tacitus can compare the effect of the payment of Roman money to him with the effect of Roman armed intervention on his behalf? And how was it that such a chief could actually acquire coercive power? The Imperial authorities would certainly have thrown their money away if they had merely bribed a single individual, a chief whose career so far from winning him popular confidence had earned him popular distrust. If the tribesmen had seen Roman gold in such a chief's personal possession without bringing any advantage to themselves they would not have submitted to his rule without ado. Nor again was the money always used to win over the warriors as a whole by open-handed and indiscriminate generosity to acquiesce in Roman policy; for Tacitus distinctly implies that the chiefs of whom he is speaking had no general support among the people.[1] We may conjecture that the chief was intended to use the money and gifts which the Romans sent him so as to increase the strength of his retinue or so as to augment the lavishness with which he supported the 'companions' who already followed him, thus binding them more closely to himself and making it probable that other young noblemen would come from among other peoples as well as his own people and attach themselves to him.[2] Granted the truth of Tacitus' implication that such chiefs were sometimes without popular support —and specific cases are known (p. 99 below)—it

[1] *G* xlii. 2. The position may, however, have been different when the sums arriving in Germany were so vast as those paid by M. Aurelius and Commodus: Bolin, art. cit. (on p. 21 n. 3 above), 134. Unfortunately, no specific information survives about the size of the sums paid over by the early Emperors to the Germans, though cf. Julian, *Ep. ad Ath.* 280 A.

[2] Tacitus, *G* v. 4, xv. 3: see Anderson, ad loc. Claudius sent Italicus home *auctum pecunia*, *A* xi. 16. 3.

follows that their power had of necessity to be coercive if they were to rule at all. In these cases, and hence potentially in all cases, the retinue was not merely a force which could be used for carrying out raids on other peoples: it was also a coercive force directed in the interests of the chief and its own members against the chief's own people. The chief's retinue was now such that he could exact obedience not because of custom or traditional usage but by virtue of his superior armed force. He could impose his 'laws', as a later chief put it. And it may well be that his authority would now extend into spheres where formerly there had been no precedent for the chief to exercise authority at all.

But once a chief embarked on this policy of strengthening his retinue by means of Roman subsidies it must have been difficult for him to turn back. His retinue was no longer based on his regular economic power, his ability to bring in a steady flow of booty, and the like. It was more artificial and precarious, depending as it did on the continued goodwill of the Roman government. The chief who spent his subsidy thus in strengthening his retinue over against his people could hardly maintain his inflated retinue on the lavish scale now possible for him unless the money arrived regularly. It was vital to his interests, perhaps even to his existence, not only himself to give no offence to the Romans but also to prevent his tribesmen from putting into effect any policy which might injure Roman interests. We never hear of a Germanic chieftain in this period who, when once he had begun to accept them, was able to spurn his subsidies, forfeit them, and turn against the Imperial government. For if these chiefs refused to accept Roman money any longer they would have had no support either from the Romans or from their own people. At all events, it now happened that some chiefs were looked upon with deep hatred by their people, but since they showed 'outstanding loyalty' to the Romans the people were not able to expel them. Vangio and Sido were of 'splendid loyalty' to Rome but were 'hated' by their followers.[1] They came to their office in A.D. 50; and nearly twenty years later Sido re-appears in history, and he is still as loyal as ever to the Romans. Vangio had disappeared in the meantime and had been replaced by a chief with the suspicious name of Italicus; and the pair continued to show the utmost loyalty to Rome.[2] This is a specific case where owing to Roman interference the people were unable to rid themselves of leaders whom they disliked. The leaders' power was based on force, and their force was derived from Roman money.

Often enough, however, the retinue was not able to protect its leader against the forces of the people and had to accompany him into exile. In A.D. 15 Germanicus had to rescue Segestes and his kindred and retinue from the fury of the Cheruscan warriors (p. 80 above): the Caesar settled them west of the Rhine, perhaps giving them land there.[3] In 18 or 19 the great Maroboduus himself was driven from among his people by a concerted effort of the nobility of the Marcomanni aided by Roman intrigue. He crossed the Danube into the province of Noricum, and the Emperor Tiberius settled him in Ravenna. When Catualda, who had played a leading part in expelling him, was himself expelled

---

[1] Ibid., xii. 30. 4. It does not necessarily follow from the words 'regnum Vangio ac Sido inter se partivere' that the two chiefs actually *divided* the kingdom, made it into two kingdoms, and proceeded to rule these two kingdoms independently: (see p. 39 n. 1 above). Rather, they are another example of the dual leadership discussed above.

[2] Tacitus, *H* iii. 5, cf. 21.    [3] Id., *A* i. 58. 8.

shortly afterwards, Tiberius settled him in Fréjus. The retinues of the two exiles were detached from them and were settled across the Danube between the rivers March and Waag. In their new home the Romans appointed as their chieftain a Quadic nobleman called Vannius (p. 92 above); and it is unfortunate that we do not know how the Roman government proposed to control him.[1] In the year 50 this Vannius was himself expelled along with his retinue, and the Emperor Claudius gave them land in Pannonia.[2] But there may have been many cases like that of Vangio and Sido where the retinues were wholly successful in keeping their unpopular leaders in power. Indeed, the retinues may have been unsuccessful in some cases only because the Romans sided against them. Catualda was helped to expel Maroboduus by Roman gold, which may also have played a part in his own overthrow a little later; for in view of the vast strength of the Marcomanni in Augustus' reign it was very much to the interests of the Romans to keep them as disturbed as possible.[3] Moreover, it is scarcely a coincidence that when Vannius was driven out he was succeeded as ruler of those of his people who did not enter Roman territory with him by Vangio and Sido, whose 'splendid loyalty' has already been mentioned. It may be, then, that when the retinues failed to give chieftains coercive power over their people this was often due in some measure to

---

[1] Ibid., ii. 62 f.

[2] Ibid., xii. 30. 3. It is thought that a Germanic grave found near Mannersdorf on the Leithagebirge may be a remnant of Vannius' settlement in Pannonia: L. Franz, *XVIII Bericht d. röm.-germ. Kommission* (1929), 138; cf. R. Egger, *Laureae Aquincenses*, i (Budapest, 1938), 147–50.

[3] Tacitus, *A* ii. 62. 1, 63. 4; Velleius, ii. 129. 3; Aur. Victor, *Caes.* ii. 4 *callide*. Catualda: see e.g. J. Klose, *Roms Klientel-Randstaaten am Rhein und an der Donau* (Breslau, 1934), 65 f., 72.

Roman interference. And when it did not suit the Romans to interfere, the people's chances of driving out an unpopular leader or optimate were not negligible.[1] Of course, the Romans did not intrigue to expel these chiefs with the aim of restoring the freedom of the old form of society nor did they appeal to the masses of the Marcomanni and the others to rid themselves of the tyrants. The instrument which they used in expelling Maroboduus was not the people at large but the nobility.[2] And the *coup* of the nobles seems to have been neither resisted nor supported by the common warriors: it is simply recorded that after the nobles had struck their blow 'Maroboduus was deserted on all sides'.[3] He was a tyrant: the people had no interest in preserving him or in assisting the nobles, and so they stood aside from the struggle.

But even when a chief was driven out by his people his usefulness to Rome had not come to an end: the Emperors did not give land to such men as Vannius and the others without having a purpose in mind. In spite of the fact that Roman machinations had actually played some part in causing Maroboduus' expulsion Tiberius provided him with a refuge at Ravenna where he lived on for eighteen years. And if at any time during those years the Marcomanni seemed likely to threaten the provinces Tiberius made as if to restore Maroboduus. The Emperor thus managed to keep the Marcomanni

---

[1] There may be an interesting history behind the third-century inscription found in or near Carnuntum on the tombstone of Septimius Aistomodius, *rex Germanorum*, i.e. of the Marcomanni or Quadi, *CIL* iii. 4453 = Dessau 856. For extreme behaviour on the part of non-Germanic peoples towards their leaders on the issue of Roman relations see Caesar, *BG* iii. 17. 3; Dio Cassius, lxxi. 16. 1. For the exile, apparently brought about by Roman intrigue, of a late-fourth-century Frankish chief see Claudian, *i cons. Stil.* 241 f.

[2] Tacitus, *A* ii. 62. 3.        [3] Ibid., 63. 1.

in a state of uncertainty and no doubt of some mutual suspicion.[1] Tiberius in fact was able to put pressure on them whenever it suited him to do so; and the use which Tiberius made of Maroboduus could equally well be made by any Roman Emperor with any nobly-born hostage or exile whom he might chance to have in his hands.

All this by no means exhausts the list of the methods by which the Roman authorities tried to control the peoples living immediately beyond the frontier. There is one such method about which we should like to have further information: they sometimes reserved to themselves the right to ratify or to refuse to ratify the choice of leader made by the people in question. Thus, they interfered with the chieftainship of the Quadi at the end of the first century (p. 94 above). Late in the second century, too, they had the right to confirm the chief of this people in his office. The choice of a certain Furtius had been thus ratified, but then the people rose against him and drove him out apparently because he had been rather too anxious to come to an agreement with the Romans. The people chose in his place one Ariogaisus. The Emperor Marcus Aurelius was so enraged at their insolence in choosing a chief to their own liking that he issued a proclamation offering a reward of 1,000 *aurei* if Ariogaisus were brought in alive and 500 *aurei* if his head could be shown.[2]

---

[1] Ibid., 63. 5; Velleius, ii. 129. 3; Suetonius, *Tib*. xxxvii. 4. Cf. the position of the Parthians in A.D. 18 when Vonones was kept in Syria by the Romans, Tacitus, *A* ii. 58. 1 'petere [sc. Artabanus] interim ne Vonones in Suria haberetur neu proceres gentium propinquis nuntiis ad discordias traheret'.

[2] Dio Cassius, lxxi. 13. 3 f., 14. 1. (Note αὐτοὶ ἐφ' ἑαυτῶν, i.e. without consultation with the Romans), cf. *SHA, Marcus* xiv. 3. It was the custom of the sixth-century Moors to recognize no ruler until the Emperor had given him the insignia of office, and this practice held even when the new

As an alternative to corrupting or controlling or dividing the leading men of the Germanic peoples Roman governments of the earlier Empire sometimes tried to carry out a complementary policy. Where for some reason a subservient chieftain was not, or could not be, imposed on a barbarian people the Romans sometimes tried to make it impossible for the democratic assemblies of the warriors to hold their meetings effectively. If subservient leaders could not be imposed, at least the primitive democracy could be hamstrung. That is why the Emperor Commodus stipulated in a treaty with the Marcomanni in 180 that the warriors should not be allowed to assemble oftener than once a month (p. 42 above), and then only at a place in their territory specified by him and in the presence of a Roman centurion. The centurion would no doubt put an abrupt stop to the discussion of any project which in his opinion might be contrary to the Imperial wishes; or at any rate he would be able to inform the Roman authorities that dangerous projects were under consideration. We do not know whether there were among the Marcomanni at this date any men who held similar ideas to those of Segestes among the Cherusci more than a century earlier. But if there were, then the interference of the centurion at the assemblies may not have been universally resented. At any rate, this was no isolated case, for the same Emperor when making certain concessions to the non-Germanic Iazyges professed himself unable to relax the conditions which he had imposed on their assembling together.[1] And it

ruler was the enemy of the Romans: Procopius, *BV* iii. 25. 5. Cf. the Lazi of Colchis, id., *BP* ii. 15. 2, and the Zechi at the eastern shore of the Black Sea, id., *BG* viii. 4. 2.

[1] Dio Cassius, lxxii. 2. 4; cf. lxxi. 19. 2. Cf. the sixth-century Lazi in Procopius, *BP* ii. 15. 21. Some also cite Tacitus, *H* iv. 64, as another

seems to have been a practice of Commodus' father Marcus Aurelius to alter the 'polity' of his barbarian enemies if he thought fit and had the power to do so.[1]

A final illustration will reveal several of these phenomena in progress and will show something of the persistence and tenacity of the Romans in their attempts to disrupt the social organization of their enemies. In A.D. 28 a rebellion broke out among the Frisians who lived east of the Rhine but were subject in some sense to Roman rule. Some forty years earlier Drusus, the conqueror of Germany, had imposed on them a small tribute of leather which could be used by the Romans for making shields, tents, and other articles of military value. They lived in circumstances of great poverty, and no close attention had been paid to the quality or the size of the ox-hides which they paid, until a centurion named Olennius, who had been appointed to supervise them, began to exact the hides with extreme rigour. In order to pay the tribute the Frisians found themselves obliged to sell their herds and lands and eventually even their wives and children. When they rebelled in 28 the pro-praetor of Lower Germany went to crush them but suffered a severe moral defeat; and the Frisians' victory brought them fame throughout Germany.[2] For twenty years they remained independent of the Romans and were either openly or potentially hostile to them. It might have been expected that if their liberty were

example; but the reference there is not to Germanic assemblies in Germany itself but to meetings of the Tencteri 'Rheno discreta gens' with the Ubii of Cologne. For a possible parallel from the third century in Scotland see I. A. Richmond and O. G. S. Crawford, *Archaeologia* xciii (1949), 15. Charlemagne applied a similar policy to the Saxons, *Cap. de Part. Saxon.* xxxiv 'interdiximus ut omnes Saxones generaliter conventus publicos nec faciant nisi forte missus noster de verbo nostro congregare fecerit'.

[1] Dio Cassius, lxxi. 19. 1 πολιτείαν.　　　[2] Tacitus, *A* iv. 72 f.

threatened again they would defend it with redoubled ardour. But in fact, when they next appear in history, in the year 47, it is recorded that they gave hostages to Domitius Corbulo, legate of Lower Germany, who removed them from their dwellings and settled them on land of his own choosing. There is no hint that they resisted him. They submitted meekly to his orders and tamely allowed him to plant garrisons among them in their new land. What had sapped their will to resist? As soon as Corbulo had settled them in their new lands, according to Tacitus, 'he imposed on them a senate, magistrates, and laws'. What this change amounted to is not known in detail, but there can be little doubt that he reconstructed their system of government, removed the old assembly, council, and war-chieftainship, and consolidated the position of the nobility in such a way as to free them substantially from control by the warriors. It may be, then, that the Frisians did not resist Corbulo because their nobles were not wholly unwilling to accept his 'constitution'.[1] In view of the general poverty of the Frisians, however, it would be easy to exaggerate the extent to which the interests of the nobility conflicted with those of the common tribesmen. At any rate, the Romans withdrew from the area shortly afterwards, and before the year 58 the Frisians, although they still appear in some measure to have been dependent on the Roman government,[2] had thrown off their new constitution and had reverted to the old system of government by assembly, council, and chiefs. For in that year, according to Tacitus, they were led by 'Verritus and Malorix, who ruled that people as kings, in so far as Germans admit of kingly rule', a phrase which refers to

---

[1] Ibid., xi. 19. 1 f.
[2] M. Bang, *Die Germanen im römischen Dienst* (Berlin, 1906), 8.

the position of the dual rulers who are so often found in the Germanic world (p. 39 above), but which by no means describes the kind of 'magistrate' whom Corbulo is likely to have imposed on them.[1] The indefatigable Romans even then tried to drive a wedge between the two leaders and the rest of the people. For when Verritus and Malorix went to Rome to try to induce Nero's government to allow them to keep some land on which they had squatted, Nero refused to agree; but he presented the two leaders with the Roman citizenship although they are not known to have given any military service to the Empire. Had not Segestes said many years before that from the day on which he had been given the Roman citizenship he had chosen his friends and enemies as suited the Roman interest? But Verritus and Malorix were not for sale. The Frisians defied Nero's orders and were only driven from the disputed lands by force.[2] And when the Ampsivarii tried a little later to occupy those same lands the Romans refused them permission to do so, but they privately offered land to their chief Boiocalus (p. 78 above).[3] In the case of peoples among whom wealth had accumulated to a greater extent than among the Frisians and Ampsivarii Nero's diplomats would have had a better chance of success.

### 3. The Tribal Nobility and the Romans

The internal history of the Germanic peoples living near the Roman frontier during the period of the early Empire turned largely on the relationship between three forces; and these forces continued to play a considerable part in Germanic history throughout the whole of the Roman period. The first of these forces is the rank

---

[1] Tacitus, *A* xiii. 54. 2; cf. Suetonius, *Claud.* xxv. 4.
[2] Tacitus, *A* xiii. 54. 6–7.    [3] Ibid., 56. 2.

and file of the Germanic warriors. These were men who generally supported the old system of social organization with its free institutions which had evolved when property was mainly communal and which allowed little scope for the increasing social power of men who held quantities of property privately. Secondly, the tribal nobility, whose social power was directly based on their retinues, tried to withdraw themselves from the control of the assembled warriors and on occasion even to subvert the assembly altogether. The old egalitarian system allowed little scope, as we have suggested, for the increasing social and economic power of the optimates. Some of the optimates, therefore, tried to revolutionize the old society and to re-fashion it in such a way as to permit them to develop their interests and exercise their power; and there were two ways in which a leading man might set about this task. He might make a violent attempt to overthrow the old institutions and to establish a personal tyranny with the aid of his retinue, his kindred, and such fellow-notables as might agree to join him. Alternatively, he might turn to the Romans. If the Romans were in occupation of his country he might support their occupation and hope for its continuance; but if they were far away he might nevertheless win the support of their influence and if possible of their wealth. The third factor is the Roman authorities, who intervened in the internal affairs of the various frontier peoples in order to support such of the leading men as they considered useful to them. They did this because deft use of the leading men might well preserve peace and protect Roman property on the frontiers and might extend Roman influence far beyond the Rhine and the Danube.

Of these three forces, then—the common warriors,

the native nobility, and the Roman government—two had sometimes much in common, for the ties which bound the retinue-leaders to the Romans were in some cases shown to be stronger than the ties which bound them to their own people. The issues may have been anything but clear-cut in the early days of the Roman Empire, the ranks of the nobility may usually have been divided, and only a small minority may have put their interest as a group before the general interest of their people. Moreover, the Roman government set very definite limits to the lengths to which it would go in defence of a 'loyal' chieftain. On the other hand, these were the men on whom Roman power had to a large extent been based east of the Rhine, and judicious handling of them could preserve much Roman influence beyond the frontier. At bottom, then, two of the three forces had, or showed some tendency to have, more in common with each other than either had with the third. Given the internal development of Germanic society with the accumulation of privately owned wealth and the consequent pressure against the old way of managing public affairs, it was all but inevitable that there should be a persistent tendency among the German nobility to look to Rome to guarantee the social position which they now claimed for themselves. This tendency existed among the German optimates throughout the whole of Imperial history and it was still stronger in the days of Theodoric II in Gaul than it had been in the time of Segestes. The question of their relations with the Roman government was often to be the dominating issue in the internal as well as in the external history of the Germanic peoples during the rest of the Roman period.

# CHAPTER FOUR

# EARLY GERMANIC WARFARE

THREE topics are discussed in the following pages: (i) weapons and tactics, (ii) siege warfare, and (iii) strategy. But it is necessary to begin by stressing the immense technical superiority of the Roman Empire over all its neighbours.

Throughout the heyday of their civilization the Romans made a comparatively small contribution to the development of mechanical techniques; but their capacity for absorbing and developing the inventions, and particularly the weapons, of others aroused widespread discussion in the ancient world and indeed became something of a commonplace in Greco-Roman literature.[1] When Roman armies first entered northwestern Europe in force, the natives of that region were astounded and often demoralized by the sheer technical ability of the invaders. Again and again in his *Gallic War* Caesar remarks on the astonishment of the Gauls, Britons, and Germans at the techniques of his troops.[2] Now, the techniques of the Gauls themselves were by no means primitive by Roman standards, and the Gauls were quick to learn from their conquerors.[3] But they

[1] See e.g. Poseidonius, 87 F 59 § 106 (Jacoby), with the discussion by E. Wendling, 'Zu Poseidonius und Varro', *Hermes*, xxviii (1893), 335–53; cf. Walbank on Polybius, i. 20. 15. But C. Schuchhardt, 'Die Römer als Nachahmer in Landtwehr- und Lagerbau', *Sitzungsber. d. preussischen Akad. d. Wissen.: phil.-hist. Klasse*, (1931), 608–34, should be read with caution.

[2] See esp. *BG* ii. 30 f. Note also i. 13. 2 (bridge-building), ii. 12. 5 (siege engines), iv. 25. 1 f. (warships and *tormenta* dismay the Britons, cf. Tacitus, *Agric.* xxv. 2), vii. 29. 2 (siege warfare); A. Hirtius, *BG* viii. 43. 4 f.

[3] Caesar, *BG* iii. 21. 3, vii. 22. 1–3, 23. 5, 29. 7, 30. 4; Diodorus Siculus, v. 31. 1 ταῖς δὲ διανοίαις ὀξεῖς καὶ πρὸς μάθησιν οὐκ ἀφυεῖς.

could only imitate what they had the technical resources to make for themselves and what their Roman
prisoners could teach them to construct (though they
might be impressive pupils);[1] and when their country
had risen in its last assault on the invaders, the Gauls
believed that they had been beaten not by Roman
courage and discipline but by Roman technical
superiority, especially in siege operations.[2]

On every frontier the barbarians suffered from this
same inferiority. The Dacians,[3] the steppe nomads,[4] and
even the great Persian Empire itself[5] were no match for
the Romans in technical achievements. Moreover, apart
from technicians and technical skill the Romans also
had at their disposal far greater quantities of the raw
materials essential to war than had any of their neighbours.[6] Consider a random entry in a late Roman
chronicle. A certain Aristus, commander of the Illyrican
troops in 499, marched out with 15,000 soldiers to fight
the Bulgars who were devastating Thrace in that year;
and he brought with him no fewer than 520 wagons

Not very long after Caesar's wars in Gaul the Romans were experi-
menting with a Celtic type of shield boss: M. Jahn, *Die Bewaffnung der
Germanen in der älteren Eisenzeit*, Mannusbibliothek xvi (Leipzig, 1916),
40 f., 47 f., a work to which I am heavily indebted.

[1] Caesar, *BG* v. 42. 1–3, 5 (cf. 52. 2), vii. 22. 1–3, 30. 4.

[2] Ibid., vii. 29. 2.

[3] Dio Cassius, lxvii. 7. 4, lxviii. 9. 3 and 5; cf. Petrus Patricius, frag. 5.

[4] See E. A. Thompson, *Attila and the Huns* (Oxford, 1948), 172 f., 180,
and add references to Theophylactus Simocatta, ii. 16. 10 f., and to
Theophanes, a.m. 6305 (p. 498, ed. de Boor). For the high value which
the Indian kings put on Roman technicians, including the makers of
siege engines, see M. P. Charlesworth, 'Roman Trade with India: A
Re-survey', apud P. R. Coleman-Norton (ed.), *Studies in Roman Economic
and Social History* (Princeton, 1951), 131–43, at 133; R. E. M. Wheeler,
*Rome Beyond the Imperial Frontiers* (London, 1954), 133 *et al.* For an
attempt to prevent the art of ship-building from reaching barbarians
who were still unfamiliar with it see *Cod. Theodos.* ix. 40. 24.

[5] See e.g. Herodian, *Hist.* iii. 4. 8 f.

[6] Two passages which will repay study in this connexion are Herodian,
*Hist.* iv. 10. 4, and Libanius, *Or.* lix. 66 ff.

loaded with the weapons alone which were essential for the campaign.[1] No other ancient State had soldiers with such 'fire-power' as these figures imply. More than half a millenium earlier Julius Caesar did not conceal the efforts which he made to impress upon the Gauls the vastness of the resources of Italy—any losses which the Romans might suffer in war could be replaced over and over again.[2]

### 1. Weapons and Tactics

Now, the Gauls, to say nothing of the Persians, had reached a higher level of material development than the Germans at the time when both alike clashed with the armies of Julius Caesar. In Caesar's time the use of iron among the Germans was severely limited, at any rate by Roman standards (p. 9 above). Indeed, it has been said that German weapons, both defensive and offensive, were characterized by poverty of metal; and Tacitus points to their weapons to prove the shortage of iron among the German communities.[3] Germanicus could encourage his men without absurd exaggeration by pointing out to them that the German warriors had neither breastplates nor helmets, that their shields were not strengthened with iron or leather but were made merely of wickerwork and thin, painted boards, and that the spears of many of them were not tipped with iron at all but were merely hardened by fire.[4]

In fact, when the German warrior, whether horseman or foot, went into battle in the first century A.D.,

[1] Marcellinus Comes, s.a. 499 (*Chronica Minora*, ii. 95).
[2] Caesar, *BG* vi. 1. 3, 4 *fin.*, though note iii. 5. 1; A. Hirtius, *BG* viii. 1. 2.
[3] H. Delbrück, *Geschichte d. Kriegskunst*, ii², (Berlin, 1921), 40; Tacitus, *Germ.* vi. 1.
[4] Id., *A* ii. 14, 3; cf. *G* vi. 1–3; cf. Dio Cassius, xxxviii. 50. 2; Herodian, *Hist.* vi. 7. 8; Agathias, *Hist.* ii. 5.

his main weapon was a long lance with one end sharpened and hardened by fire, or else fitted with a short narrow iron point, which could be hurled or used for thrusting.[1] Some foot-soldiers also had several spears each which they could throw;[2] but only a handful of them—the more well-to-do—could afford to carry a sword in addition.[3] These offensive weapons left them at an inferiority to the Romans. For while the lances and spears might possibly match the Roman *pilum* (which, of course, was not a thrusting weapon), the German sword was found wanting (quite apart from the fact that the majority of Germanic warriors possessed no sword at all): swords appear to have been used much less frequently in the early Roman period, even by those who could afford to own them, than had been the case before the Germans came in contact with the Romans. In some measure the sword as such was found to be an unsatisfactory weapon in warfare against the Romans. When their defensive armour was so scanty it was advisable to use a long thrusting spear and so to keep one's distance rather than to use a sword and so be forced to come to grips with the heavily clad Romans.[4]

In their defensive armour the Germans were at a disastrous disadvantage to the Imperial troops. They

[1] Tacitus, *A* ii. 14. 4, *G* vi. 1 (which is confirmed by the archaeological evidence); Plutarch, *Marius* xxv. 7 (though the iron breastplates of that passage are sometimes thought to have been booty taken from the Gauls). The great length of the Germanic spear is emphasized by Tacitus, *A* i. 64. 3, ii. 14. 3, 21. 1, *H* v. 18; cf. Amm. Marc. xvii. 12. 2 (Sarmatians and Quadi). On some relevant representations in Roman art see P. G. Hamberg, *Acta Archaeologica*, vii (1936), 21–49, and esp. Jahn, op. cit.

[2] Tacitus, *G* vi. 2, *H* v. 17; SHA, *Claudius* viii. 5.

[3] Tacitus, *G* vi. 1.

[4] So Jahn, op. cit. The Caledonians, too, had reason to know that a long sword without a point was of little use in close hand-to-hand encounters with the Romans: Tacitus, *Agr.* xxxvi. 1, where it is to be noted that the Caledonians' enemies are Germans.

went into battle either naked or wearing only a short cloak.[1] Helmets and breastplates were practically unknown.[2] Their only defensive weapon was the light wooden or wicker shield which Germanicus spoke of with contempt. But these shields were not used only to parry their opponents' blows or to deflect their missiles: they were fitted with an iron boss sometimes as much as twelve centimetres high and so fashioned that the shield became a thrusting weapon in itself. Their smiths showed almost endless initiative in working out independently of Celtic or Roman influences new types of boss which would make a thrust of the shield more effective.[3] But in fact the shield of wickerwork or light boards (sometimes fitted with an iron rim) was as a rule only half a centimetre thick at the edges and one to one and a half centimetre round the boss in the centre;[4] and even when it was strengthened with leather—for Germanicus exaggerated when he said that this was not done—it could easily be smashed by the adversary's steel. In all, we can hardly hesitate to agree with an historian of the sixth century A.D. who, having occasion to comment on the arms and armour of the Germans, says that their armament was paltry and such as would

---

[1] Id., *G* vi. 2, *H* ii. 22; cf. Dio Cassius, xxxviii. 45. 4; Herodian, *Hist.* vi. 7. 8. Even in the sixth century the Frankish and Herul warriors fought naked from the waist up: Agathias, *Hist.* ii. 5; Paulus Diaconus, *HL* i. 20 (though the Heruls in Procopius, *BP* ii. 25. 27, wear a short cloak). This, of course, was not a German peculiarity; cf. Livy, xxii. 46. 6 (Gauls); Procopius, *BG* vii. 14. 26 (Slavs and Antae); etc.

[2] Tacitus, *G* vi. 3. According to Hamberg, art. cit. 24, in the whole of Roman *Triumphalkunst* not a single German (apart from some in Roman service) is represented as wearing helmet or armour.

[3] Jahn, op. cit. 152 ff. For a vivid representation see Hamberg, art. cit. 30, with Abbildung 4; and note J. Dobiáš, 'Roman Imperial Coins as a Source for Germanic Antiquities', *Transactions of the International Numismatic Congress, London 1936* (London, 1938), 160–78, who discusses the German shield on 161–9.

[4] Jahn, op. cit. 164 f., 182, 201 ff.; Hamberg, art. cit. 28.

need no skilled technicians to repair if it were damaged: repairs could be carried out by the warriors themselves.[1]

All this explains the need for that swift, wild rush in their wedge-shaped formations[2] with which the Germans would charge the ranks of their heavily armed opponents. Their only hope of overwhelming a Roman commander in open country, clear of their own woods and marshes, was to break his line by the impetus of their first attack; and on at least one occasion their charge was so headlong as to leave the Roman troops no time to hurl their javelins at all.[3] They attacked of necessity: they dared not wait to be attacked. (It was advisable, of course, to avoid the error of judgement of which some of Caesar's enemies were guilty, who charged so rapidly over such a long distance that when at last they arrived at the Roman lines they were panting and breathless and quite unable to fight a battle.)[4] But if the Germans were caught up and entangled in a prolonged hand-to-hand grapple where their light shield and thrusting-spear were confronted with the heavy metal helmet, breastplate, and shield, and the steel sword of the Romans, their personal bravery would often avail them little[5] This was particularly the case since many of them, when once they chose or were compelled to hurl their spears, would be left without any weapon of any kind, offensive or defensive, apart from their heavily bossed shields—unless they could pick up a

[1] Agathias, loc. cit.

[2] H. G. Gundel, *Untersuchungen zur Taktik und Strategie der Germanen*, Diss. Marburg, 1937, 8. On the *cuneus* see Fiebiger, P.-W. iv. 1756 f.; Delbrück, op. cit. ii. 32 ff., 43 ff.; Gundel, op. cit. 11–18. How the various *comitatus* fitted into, or alongside, the *cunei* is unknown.

[3] Caesar, *BG* i. 52. 3, but the Romans charged simultaneously.

[4] Caesar, *BG* ii. 23. 1, iii. 19. 1. It was a tactic to induce the enemy to do this: id., *BC* iii. 92. 3.

[5] Tacitus, *A* ii. 21. 1 'nec minor Germanis animus, sed genere pugnae et armorum superabantur', etc.; cf. Gundel, op. cit., 35, 39 f.

spear which had already been thrown[1] or unless they chose to pick up stones and throw them: we even hear of German *horsemen* throwing stones.[2] The fact is that in open battle against Roman legionaries the Germanic warriors were little, if at all, more effective than the Achaean heroes of Homer would have been (except that what metal weapons they had were made of iron and not bronze). It was useless to fight the Imperial armies with the tactics and equipment of Achilles and Agamemnon, which even in A.D. 552 the last Ostrogothic king of Italy employed in his last battle against the Romans.[3] As a rule it was also useless for the Germans to fight the Roman invaders inside the forests of their country. There, as Germanicus told his men (and he soon proved it in action), among the trees and undergrowth the advantage would have lain with the Romans. If the mass of the warriors were closely crowded together among the trees, the German's long lance became unwieldy, he could not run to pick up a lance or other weapon lying on the ground, and he could not exploit his fleetness of foot: he merely stood defenceless for the legionaries to cut him down.[4] But if they could not fight successfully either in the open or in the woods, what were they to do? The Germans solved this problem to some extent by catching the Romans, whenever it was possible, on an open plain surrounded by woods (or marshes) and by launching incessant, sharp, and short attacks on them from all directions using the woods as cover.[5]

[1] Tacitus, loc. cit. *colligeret.*     [2] Caesar, *BG* i. 46. 1; Tacitus, *H* v. 17.
[3] Procopius, *BG* viii. 35. 20 ff.     [4] Tacitus, *A* ii. 14.3, 21. 1.
[5] Ibid., i. 63.1 ff., ii. 11. 3 (Cheruscan tactics against Chariovalda's Batavians), 16. 1 ff., 19. 3; Frontinus, *Strateg.* i. 3. 10 (which probably refers, however, to the strategy of German raids rather than to the tactics of the Germans in battle), ii. 3. 23; *SHA, Aurelian* xxi. 2 f.; Herodian,

German cavalry was somewhat less ineffective than German infantry, and from Caesar's day onwards German horsemen were frequently used in the Roman army.[1] But their number was severely limited, for only a few Germans could afford to keep a horse: the cavalry were in general identical with the nobles.[2] Moreover, at a later date, when the Germans were using bows and arrows (with which they began to arm themselves extensively in the third century A.D.),[3] their ability to fight the Romans inside the forests was somewhat increased.[4] But from the point of view of weapons the position of the Germans had improved only slightly in the late Roman period. How, for example, were the Visigoths armed when they engaged the Emperor Valens at Adrianople? What is known of their warfare in general does not suggest that their main strength lay in their cavalry. It is true that their nobility were mounted[5] (on horses which were inferior to Roman

---

*Hist.* vii. 2. 5 f. In Tacitus, *A* ii. 14. 3, Germanicus tells his men that 'non campos modo militi Romano ad proelium bonos, sed si ratio adsit, silvas et saltus', but cf. i. 64. 3, ii. 5. 3, *H* v. 17 (marshes).

[1] Caesar, *BG* iv. 12; Tacitus, *H* iv. 20. Note also Plutarch, *Otho* xii; Dio Cassius, lv. 24. 7. On German cavalry and a typically Roman use of it see Herodian, *Hist.* viii. 1. 3; cf. Delbrück, op. cit. ii. 432 ff.

[2] Those who will, may follow A. Alföldi, *Cambridge Ancient History*, xii. 159, in supposing that 'there is probably no great exaggeration' in the statement of Dexippus, 100 F 6 § 4 (Jacoby), that the Iuthungi could put 40,000 horse into the field. But Dexippus does not suggest that the Iuthungi were an essentially cavalry power.

[3] Jahn, op. cit. 57, 87. J. Werner, 'Pfeilspitzen aus Silber und Bronze in germanischen Adelsgräbern der Kaiserzeit', *Historisches Jahrbuch*, lxxiv (1955), 38–41, at 40, suggests that the use of the bow may have become customary among the Germans after the wars with M. Aurelius: the Germans would have noted the effectiveness of the Sarmatian and Iazygian archers. I am not sure that this is convincing, but can suggest nothing better.

[4] e.g. Greg. Tur. *HF* ii. 9, p. 53, ed. Krusch (1937).

[5] No more than this can be safely deduced from Amm. Marc. xxxi. 5. 7, 7. 13, 8. 10; Zosimus, iv. 22. 1; cf. Olympiodorus, frag. 26; Claudian, *In Rufin.* ii. 80, *vi cons. Hon.* 225 f., 240, 284, *BG* 192, 216 f.

horses),[1] but the army was still essentially an army
of infantrymen. These infantrymen still used the
spears which had always been the chief weapon of the
Germans,[2] and they used axes and clubs hardened by
fire,[3] which may or may not have been impromptu
weapons used only because the mass of the people had
been disarmed in 376 and had not yet succeeded in re-
arming themselves fully. They also used bows and
arrows tipped with iron (though these were not in any
sense their characteristic weapons),[4] and their horsemen, i.e. their nobility, had a long two-edged cavalry
sword adapted from the sword which was used by the
Sarmatians and Alans of the Pontic region.[5] There is no
reason to think that Fritigern's men had appreciably
greater quantities of metal at their disposal than
Arminius' warriors had had 350 years earlier. On the
other hand, we cannot suppose that they were a more

[1] Orosius, vii. 34. 5; Zosimus, iv. 22. 1–3. German horses had been
unimpressive in the early Roman period, too: p. 4 n. 1 above. But in
the sixth century German horses began to win some renown: see R. Much
on Tacitus, *G* vi. 3.

[2] Amm. Marc., xxxi. 5. 9, 7. 12, 13, 13. 1; Orosius, vii. 33. 14 *contis*; cf.
*SHA*, *Claudius* viii. 5. For Jordanes, *Get.* 261, *conti* were the characteristic
weapons of the Goths (though he is thinking of Ostrogoths).

[3] Amm. Marc., xxxi. 7. 12, 13. 3. At the battle of Hastings some of the
English were armed with *lignis imposita saxa*; William of Poitiers, ii. 17
(p. 188, ed. Foreville).

[4] Amm. Marc., xxxi. 13. 1; cf. Orosius, vii. 33. 14 *nubibus sagittarum*;
Claudian, *In Rufin.* ii. 80, *i cons. Stil.* 111; Vegetius, i. 20. King Theodoric
II was a good bowman, Sidonius, *Ep.* i. 2. 5. Gundel, op. cit. 28, seems to
overemphasize the importance of the bow to the East German cavalrymen of the fourth century.

[5] Visigothic swords are mentioned in Amm. Marc., xxxi. 5. 9, 7.
12–13; Orosius, vii. 33. 14; cf. *SHA*, *Claudius* viii. 5. On the Gothic sword
see esp. E. Behmer, *Das zweischneidige Schwert der germanischen Völkerwanderungszeit* (Stockholm, 1939), 17 ff., 69 ff. But the only Visigothic
(as distinct from Ostrogothic) sword known from this period, so far as I
am aware, is a two-edged one with a blade of 72 cm. and a handle of
10 cm. which was found at Sântana de Mures before the systematic
excavations began there: see I. Kovacs, *Dolgozatok: Travaux de la section
numismatique et archéologique du musée national de Transylvanie à Kolozsvar*,
iii (1912), 250–367, at 361, with Figure 103 no. 3, p. 324.

primitive people than the Germans of whom Tacitus speaks; and so we may take it as certain that some, though perhaps not very many, of the Visigoths at Adrianople wore breastplates and helmets. There is no evidence, however, for the traditional view that the battle of Adrianople was a great cavalry victory. Although Ostrogothic cavalry took a decisive part in the struggle,[1] Adrianople in fact was a victory of Visigothic infantrymen over Roman infantrymen. Again, it might be thought that a people who try to defend their country by building a wall around it in the middle of a campaign, as the Visigoths did when the Huns attacked them in 376, are not a nation of horsemen.[2] The fact is that few, if any, German peoples before the sixth century are known to have relied mainly on cavalry in times of war.[3] It is true that Aurelius Victor, *Caes.* xxi. 2, describes the Alamanni as 'a numerous people who fight wonderfully on horseback': but we must beware of such facile generalizations. What Aurelius Victor really means is that the Alamannic *nobles* were good horsemen —the bulk of the Alamanni fought on foot, like the bulk of all Germanic peoples before the fifth or sixth century A.D.[4]

Another point calls for discussion. The Visigoths set

[1] Amm. Marc., xxxi. 12. 12 and 17, mentions only Ostrogothic and Alanic cavalry, and Orosius, vii. 33. 13 f., confirms that their role was a decisive one.

[2] Amm. Marc., xxxi. 3. 7. Observe that this wall differed from the walls or embankments which were constructed by some of the Germans of the first century A.D.: the latter were intended to be permanent structures designed as definitive boundary lines between the various peoples' lands, whereas the Visigoths built their wall in 376 in the middle of a campaign so as to meet the special circumstances of the Huns' atack. It was an *ad hoc* construction of purely tactical value.

[3] Cf. Tacitus, *G* xxxii. 2 ff., on the Tencteri.

[4] Cf. Amm. Marc., xvi. 12. 34. There is no valid reason for doubting the incident recounted there by Ammianus: *contra*, Delbrück, op. cit. ii, 280, followed by Gundel, op. cit. 59.

foot on Roman soil in 376 without food and largely
without weapons;[1] and the process of re-arming the
Visigothic people was not completed until the end of
the century, when they compelled the State arms fac-
tories of Illyricum to supply them with Roman weapons
and with iron.[2] In the years immediately following 376
we hear repeatedly that the Visigoths took every opportunity of obtaining Roman arms. Sometimes after an
encounter with Roman forces they would strip the
Roman wounded and dead of their armour and weapons.
Once, the defenders of a besieged city noticed that the
Visigoths were using the actual weapons which had
been hurled at them from the city walls a moment before. It looks as though the battle of Adrianople were
won by men who had to a considerable extent armed
themselves from the enemy.[3] The position of the Visigoths in the desperate years 376–8 was, of course, exceptional, for they had been disarmed at the frontier in
376. Yet it is noteworthy that in the third-century raids
they are also reported as looting weapons at Chalcedon;
and on that occasion there is no reason to doubt that
they had set out on their venture as fully equipped in
weapons and armour as they were capable of making
themselves.[4] Moreover, we more than once hear that in
the period of the early Empire, too, the Germans
equipped themselves by stripping the Roman dead

[1] Eunapius, frag. 42 (p. 238. 13 and 28, ed. Dindorf); cf. Claudian,
*BG* 533 ff. The view that they did not surrender their weapons (Jerome,
*Chron.* s.a. 3381; Orosius, vii. 33. 10) was in my opinion designed to
account for their success at Adrianople. It was true only in so far as some
Visigoths bribed the Romans to permit them to keep their arms (cf.
Eunapius, frag. 42, p. 239. 8; Zosimus, iv. 20. 6).
[2] Claudian, loc. cit.
[3] Amm. Marc., xxxi. 5. 9, 6. 3, 15. 11; cf. Orosius, vii. 34. 5. For a
case where a Roman force had to arm itself from the barbarians see
Eugippius, *Vita S. Severini* iv. 2–4.
[4] Zosimus, i. 34. 3.

after a battle.[1] The fact that Roman weapons were so often stolen or picked up during a raid may perhaps be no more than a tribute to the superior make of Roman weapons over barbarian ones. But it is tempting to ask whether the Germans were able to equip themselves fully even with their own inferior weapons for a prolonged, distant, and full-scale campaign (as distinct from a fleeting frontier raid). No German chief could begin a campaign with 520 wagon-loads of weapons like Aristus in 499 (p. 110 above). The nomads of the Eurasian steppe could not manufacture enough weapons to supply their own needs in times of full-scale warfare.[2] Even the Romans themselves had difficulties in this respect. The reader will recall how often in the first three books of Tacitus' *Histories*, where great armies are on the move, the historian turns aside to mention the manufacture or the requisitioning of arms: when the civil wars broke out, the various armies apparently had insufficient stocks to see themselves comfortably through their campaigns.[3] Now, the quantity of metal and the number of skilled smiths at the disposal of the German peoples could easily be thought greater than it in fact was. For example, at one point in their war with the Emperor Commodus the Buri were actually obliged to beg the Emperor again and again for a truce in order that they might re-arm themselves before resuming the struggle.[4] Accordingly, throughout Roman history competent Roman generals, when dealing with peoples of low technical capacity, were nearly always insistent in a

[1] Tacitus, *A* ii. 45. 4, *H* iv. 17.     [2] Thompson, op. cit. 172, 180.

[3] Tacitus, *H* i. 57, 64, 66, ii. 19, 52, 82, 84, iii. 36.

[4] Dio Cassius, lxxii. 3. 1. Note that before the war of 52 B.C. Vercingetorix prescribed the quantity of arms which each *civitas* should make in preparation for the forthcoming campaign: Caesar, *BG* vii. 4. 8. It may be doubted whether many Germanic chieftains in the first two centuries A.D. had sufficient personal power to rise to this height of organization.

moment of victory that the enemy should surrender all his weapons.[1] Primitive though the weapons were, the means of producing them were equally primitive; and the process of re-arming might be very prolonged even in peace-time.

When we turn to the sixth century A.D. we find fortunately that weapons were a subject which keenly interested Procopius; and indeed he discusses them in the very first chapter of his History. When he comes to describe the great siege of Rome by the Ostrogoths in 537–8, he turns aside to draw attention to the question of the barbarians' armament. Witigis, he says, failed to notice the difference between his men and the Romans in equipment and in military practice.[2] The Romans and their Hunnish allies were nearly all mounted archers (ἱπποτοξόται). The Ostrogoths had cavalry, and they had archers: but their archers were not their cavalrymen. The Ostrogothic cavalrymen were armed only with spears and swords, while their archers fought on foot. Hence, if the barbarian cavalry failed to get to close quarters with the foe, they had no defence against his arrows—they could not fight *eminus*—while the barbarian infantry, although armed with bows, could scarcely advance against heavy horse.[3] Unlike Witigis, Belisarius was quick to notice this fundamental difference and to see that his possession of mounted archers outweighed his inferiority in numbers.[4] What made the position worse from the Ostrogothic point of view was that their warriors do not seem to have had protective armour to safeguard them from Roman arrows. It is true that Procopius occasionally turns aside to say that

---

[1] In Caesar alone see *BG* i. 27. 3, ii. 13. 1, 15. 2, esp. 31. 3 f. with 32. 1; iii. 21. 3, vii. 11. 2, 12. 2, 89. 4; cf. Dio Cassius, liv. 31. 3, lxxii. 2. 2 f., etc.
[2] *BG* v. 27. 15.     [3] Ibid., v. 27. 27 f.     [4] Ibid., v. 27. 26.

such-and-such an Ostrogoth was armed with a helmet
and breastplate; but the mere fact that he sometimes
finds this worthy of mention suggests that such an Ostrogoth was exceptional and that in general the Ostrogothic nobility alone had satisfactory defensive armour.[1]
And even such defensive armour as they possessed would
scarcely give the Ostrogothic optimates adequate pro-
tection, for, according to Procopius, the Roman (unlike
the Persian) mounted archers fired their arrows with
such force as to be able to penetrate a shield or breastplate.[2] On the other hand, the Roman mounted archer
(again unlike the Persian) was himself equipped with a
breastplate and greaves. He carried his arrows on his
right side, and a sword on his left. Some of them also
had a spear and a small shield slung around their
shoulder to protect the face and neck. They could fire
their arrows when their horses were at full gallop, both
when they were pursuing and when they were being
pursued, and hence were able to meet new tactical
situations the moment they arose. The price which they
paid was that they were not able to discharge their
arrows so quickly as the Persian horsemen.[3] In short,
the war of the Byzantines and the Ostrogoths was
largely a struggle between heavily-armed mounted
archers and light-armed mounted spearmen (ἱππακον-
τίσται, though I do not think that Procopius ever uses

[1] See ibid., v. 22. 4, 23. 9, vi. 5. 14, vii. 4. 21. The view that Witigis'
army consisted of 150,000 horse and foot, most of them τεθωρακισμένοι,
at the beginning of the war (Procopius, BG v. 16. 11, 24. 3, vii. 21. 4) is
fantastic: see J. B. Bury, History of the Later Roman Empire[2] (London,
1923), ii. 181 n. 2.

[2] Procopius, BP i. 1. 15, is a trustworthy eye-witness and his evidence
cannot be doubted with Delbrück, op. cit. ii. 370 f., merely on the
grounds of what Dio Cassius, xl. 22, had said 300 years earlier. The
speed with which the Persians could fire their arrows is mentioned more
than once by Mauricius, Strateg. xi. 2.

[3] Procopius, BP i. 1. 11 ff., 18. 32–4; cf. BG viii. 8. 34.

this latter term). At what date the Ostrogoths and (as we shall see) the Vandals learned to become a predominantly cavalry power is a puzzle to which there does not seem to be a satisfactory answer. Darkó's view that they mounted themselves as a result of their contact with the Huns and other nomadic pastoralists in the fifth century is hardly convincing, for if they modelled themselves on mounted archers why did they turn out in the end to be mounted spearmen?[1]

\The disadvantages under which the Ostrogoths fought Belisarius, then, were very great; and they were intensified at the battle of Taginae by astonishing tactical errors (as we are told) on the part of their commander.[2] Procopius makes two criticisms of Totila's dispositions at this battle. First, the king placed his infantry in a body behind the cavalry so that the latter might have a safe retreat if they were forced to give ground. This was not a bad motive, especially if the king was unsure of his infantry—and Belisarius himself had done much the same thing in a battle outside Rome.[3] But as it turned out, the Ostrogothic cavalry, unsupported by their infantrymen's archery and relying only on their own spears, were routed, and they swept the infantry with them in their flight.[4] Perhaps the historian would have done better to criticize the Ostrogothic cavalry rather than the king personally. At any rate, the Romans exploited the individual qualities of their infantry and

[1] E. Darkó, 'Influences touraniennes sur l'évolution de l'art militaire des grecs, des romains, et des byzantins', *Byzantion* x (1935), 443–69, xii (1937), 119–47, at xii, 142. Observe that Vegetius, i. 20, explicitly says that the arms of Roman cavalry benefitted from study of those of the Goths, Alans, and Huns.

[2] On this battle see esp. Delbrück, op. cit. ii, 374–86; Bury, op. cit. ii, 261–9, 288–91.

[3] Procopius, *BG* v. 28. 22 ff.; cf. vi. 1. 2, viii. 8. 16.

[4] Ibid., viii. 32. 17.

their cavalry in the battle, and made the best use of them both. Their tactics were more elastic and less mechanical than those of the Ostrogoths.[1] Secondly, Totila gave the strange order to his men that they should not use bows and arrows or any other weapon except their spears. There is an extraordinary similarity between this and the order given by the Vandal king Gelimer to his army at the battle of Tricamarum. The Vandals, too, were not good infantrymen or archers or javelin-throwers. They fought on horseback with spear and sword and with little or no defensive armour; and so they found it difficult to come to grips with an enemy of *Fernkämpfer*.[2] Their army, in fact, was very like that of the Ostrogoths, though perhaps the latter had a larger force of infantry. How, then, are we to explain the fact that at Tricamarum Gelimer instructed all the Vandals to use their swords only, and not their spears or any other weapon?[3] Procopius emphasizes the folly of Totila's similar order at Taginae, but he makes no comment on Gelimer's order and offers no explanation of it. The fact that both kings alike instructed their men to disregard their bows and arrows suggests that there was some reason behind the order: it was not a mere personal whim, one might think, on the part of Gelimer or Totila, as we might be tempted to believe if only one of the kings had issued the order. Perhaps the aim was to do everything possible to induce their followers to

[1] Ibid., 7.
[2] Id., *BV* iii. 8. 27. Vandal cavalry is mentioned by Sidonius, *carm.* v. 398 f., 413, 423, and frequently in Procopius. On their lack of defensive armour see L. Schmidt, *Geschichte d. Wandalen*[2] (Munich, 1942), 165 n. 4. There is no valid reason for doubting Procopius' statement that the Vandals did not use the bow effectively: Procopius was an eye-witness, and weapons and tactics were matters that interested him. *Contra*, C. Courtois, *Les Vandales et l'Afrique* (Paris, 1955), 231 n. 8.
[3] Procopius, *BV* iv. 3. 9 and 14.

come to close quarters with the Roman cavalry and to allow no one an excuse for hanging back in the distance. The Romans, on the other hand, at the battle of Taginae exploited the individual qualities of their various weapons—arrows, spears, swords, etc.—and made the best use of them all.[1] In the battle itself, as it turned out, Roman *un*mounted archers inflicted decisive losses both of men and of horses on the Ostrogoths before they could even come to grips with their opponents.[2]

We have no description of the armament of the Visigoths of Spain in the sixth century. We have seen reason above to doubt the view that in the fourth century they were essentially a mounted force. As for the fifth century, a tantalizing fragment of Merobaudes tells of both infantry and cavalry in the Visigothic army in 436. Aetius routed a large force of Visigothic infantry at the Mons Colubrarius in southern Gaul and cut down their cavalry, which seems to have been less numerous. But unfortunately, this Visigothic force, which Aetius defeated, was only a detachment of king Theodoric's army, so that we do not know whether the predominance of infantry was characteristic of the army as a whole or only of this part of it.[3] In the seventh century, however, the evidence is explicit: Isidore of Seville informs us that although the Visigoths had both infantry and cavalry their main strength lay in the latter, and

[1] Id., *BG* viii. 32. 6 ff.
[2] Ibid., 10. The Ostrogothic cavalry was peculiarly ineffective against Roman infantry even when the latter was not equipped with bows and arrows: cf. their ignominious defeat in *BG* viii. 29. 16 ff.
[3] Merobaudes, *Paneg.* i, frag. ii B, p. 10. 16 ff., ed. Vollmer. In *Paneg.* ii. 158 f., p. 17, a force of besieged Visigoths has shields, spears, swords, and (last in the list) arrows. But we cannot press a poet's words on such a subject. Small groups of Visigothic cavalry are mentioned by Sidonius, *Ep.* iii. 3. 7.

their chief weapons were the spear and the javelin.[1] King Erwig in his great army law published in 681 specifies that the Visigothic landowners must bring one-tenth (or, according to some manuscripts, one half) of their slaves with them to battle;[2] and these slaves, according to the king, must not be unarmed, but must be provided with a variety of weapons: some must have *zabae* or breastplates (Erwig cannot expect *all* to have defensive armour),[3] and most of them must have shields, *spathae*, *scramae*, spears, and arrows.[4] Arrows are mentioned last in the list (though in a subsequent list slings are named, too); and perhaps it would not be rash to conclude that in the sixth and seventh centuries the Visigothic army did not differ in any important respect from the armies of Witigis and Gelimer.[5] Hence, the Visigothic kings were hard put to it to rid Spain of the Byzantines, whom Athanagild had invited into his country in 552.[6] No doubt they found the mounted archers of Byzantium as difficult to deal with as the

[1] *Chronica Minora*, ii. 294 f., cf. C. Sánchez-Albornoz, 'La Cabellería Visigoda', *Wirtschaft und Kultur: Festschrift Alfons Dopsch* (Leipzig, 1938), 92–108, at 102, 107 n. 2.

[2] On the type of army which this regulation implies see E. Oldenburg, *Die Kriegsverfassung der Westgoten*, Diss. Berlin, 1909, 50 f.

[3] See Du Cange s. vv. *zaba*, *zava*, and add to his references Mauricius, *Strateg.* xi. 2, xii. 23.

[4] *Legg. Visig.* ix. 2. 9, p. 377, ed. Zeumer.

[5] Excavation in Spain has revealed disappointingly little about Visigothic weapons: it was characteristic of the Visigoths throughout the whole of their history not to bury weapons with their dead. Only a couple of swords, some spears, and a few *scramae* have been found: see H. Zeiss, *Die Grabfunde aus dem spanischen Westgotenreich*, Germanische Denkmäler der Völkerwanderungszeit, Bd. ii (Berlin and Leipzig, 1934), 64–6, but according to Sánchez-Albornoz, art. cit. 102, some horse-trappings have also been found. The coins throw some light on the Visigothic helmet, which was very expensive and can only have been worn by the king and the nobles: see W. Reinhart, 'Germanische Helme in westgotischen Münzbildern', *Jahrbuch für Numismatik und Geldgeschichte*, ii (1950–1), 43–6.

[6] On this date see E. Stein, *Histoire du Bas-empire* (Paris, 1949), ii, 820 f.

Ostrogoths had found them. And in spite of the efforts of so powerful a king as Leovigild (568–86) the Visigoths were not able to expel the Byzantines from Spain until 624, during the troubled days of the Emperor Heraclius, when the East Roman military power had been exhausted by struggles elsewhere.

In the sixth century, then, the Germans of the Mediterranean kingdoms used the bow far more frequently than their ancestors had done in Tacitus' day. Moreover, a higher proportion of them were mounted than had been the case when Tacitus had noted that their main strength lay in their infantry: the riches of Italy, Africa, and Spain made it possible for a larger number of Germans to keep a horse, and so in the kingdoms of those countries the cavalry was the main arm. These were advances over the conditions of the first century A.D., but in the matter of defensive armour little progress seems to have been made. But it was above all their failure to combine their cavalry and their archers so as to form an adequate force of mounted archers that was the chief tactical reason for their military failures. This shortcoming is particularly surprising in the case of the Ostrogoths. When they left the low-lying area around the mouth of the Vistula *c.* A.D. 150— they had been living there since the beginning of the Christian era—they expanded over vast regions of south-eastern Europe and they must have performed the very difficult feat of adapting themselves in some measure to life on the steppe. Organization, equipment, strategy, and tactics, which had availed them in their local wars at the mouth of the Vistula, could hardly have brought them their far-flung conquests on the open plains. To have won these enormous territories in such conditions is an unsurpassed achievement in early

German history.[1] They had many opportunities of seeing the virtues of the mounted archer, but they failed to learn the lesson. And they paid the price for their failure *c.* 370, when the Huns attacked them and again when Belisarius landed in Italy.

When we turn to the Franks we find an entirely different style of warfare. Mounted archers, whether heavily armed or lightly armed, were unknown among them. The king and his immediate entourage were mounted warriors armed with spears; but these were only a small minority of the whole host. The characteristic Frankish warriors were infantrymen and were not armed with bows and arrows or spears, the only offensive weapons (apart from swords) known to the Goths and the Vandals. Each man had a sword, a shield, and a stout, sharp, iron, double-headed axe with a very short wooden handle. At the beginning of a battle the Frankish warriors threw these axes at a given signal and tried to break the enemy's shields and kill his men.[2]

---

[1] M. Rostovtzeff, *Iranians and Greeks in Southern Russia* (Oxford, 1922), 216 *et al.*, believes that the speedy conquest of the shores of the Black Sea by the Goths was facilitated by the fact that the Dnieper basin had been gradually occupied by German tribes in the first century B.C. and the first two centuries A.D. But even allowing this early German occupation of the Dnieper area (which seems very doubtful), it still remains to show (a) how those early Germans overcame the nomads of the steppe, and (b) how the Goths overcame the Germans who had been strong enough to conquer the nomads. Incidentally, in spite of W. Ensslin, *Theoderich der Grosse* (Munich, 1947), 9, and others, there is neither evidence nor likelihood that Ermanaric's empire stretched to the Volga: its boundary was the Don.

[2] Procopius, *BG* vi. 25. 2–4; cf. 12, Sidonius, *Paneg. Maior.* 237 ff. The Franks in Agathias, *Hist.* i. 14 f., ii. 5, have swords, spears, and axes. Libanius, *Or.* lix. 131, mentions their δοράτια. Battle-axes were not wholly unknown among the Goths: Amm. Marc., xxxi. 13. 3; Agathias, *Hist.* i. 9 (p. 154. 10, ed. Dindorf); and perhaps Procopius, *BP* ii. 21. 7. The western sources bearing on Frankish warfare are cited in O. M. Dalton, *The History of the Franks by Gregory of Tours* (Oxford, 1927), 225–243, though his citation of the Byzantines is incomplete. On Frankish weapons see above all E. Salin, *La Civilisation mérovingienne*, iii (Paris, 1957).

They would throw their *angones* at enemy cavalry.[1] The Franks are said to have expected in 539 that this type of fighting would overwhelm even the army of Belisarius at the first clash,[2] but they were mistaken, for the Byzantines were easily able to out-general them.[3] But the Franks, too, only rarely possessed breastplates, greaves, and helmets.[4] The decisive battle of Vouillé in 507, then, where the Franks overthrew the Gallic kingdom of the Visigoths, represented not only a victory of Franks over Visigoths but also a victory of infantry over cavalry and of the axe over the spear.[5] But the significance of this point could easily be exaggerated, for although Clovis' victory could hardly have been more complete, and although Childebert successfully invaded Spain in 531, yet the Franks were never able to defeat the Visigoths in the two centuries between 507 and 711 (when the Visigoths were overwhelmed by the Muslims). They never succeeded in wresting Septimania from the Spanish kingdom during that period, and when they interfered in Spanish affairs the Visigoths always repulsed them with vigour.[6]

According to what Procopius tells us, it would seem

---

[1] Agathias, *Hist.* i. 21 *fin.* On *angones* see n. 4 below.

[2] Procopius, *BG* vi. 28. 10; cf. Agathias, i. 7 (p. 152, 13 ff., Dindorf).

[3] See esp. Agathias, i. 21 f., ii. 8 f.

[4] Agathias, ii. 5, who confirms Procopius' description of Frankish warfare. He differs from him only in saying that the Frankish warrior carried a spear or *ango* with a barb on either side of the blade, i. 21 *fin.*, ii. 5. A similar general picture is given by Mauricius, *Strateg.* xi. 4 (p. 269 f., ed. Scheffer), who, like Agathias, *Hist.* i. 21 f., mentions their cavalry as well as their infantry.

[5] Studies of this important battle have been devoted to the site rather than to the character of the struggle, as e.g. A. F. Lièvre, 'Le lieu de la rencontre des Francs et les Wisigoths sur les bords du Clain en 507', *Revue historique*, lxvi (1898), 90–104; G. Kurth, 'La bataille de Vouillé en 507', *Revue des questions historiques*, N.S. xx (1898), 172–80.

[6] See e.g. John of Biclaro, s.a. 585 (*Chronica Minora*, ii, 217); Julianus, *Hist. Wambae* viii; *Vitas SS. Patrum Emeretensium*, v. 12. 3 (ed. J. N. Garvin, Washington, 1946).

that the further we go from the Mediterranean towards the north-west, the less important cavalry becomes. Beyond the English Channel and the Rhine cavalry played an even smaller part than it did among the Franks. The Warni were all infantrymen.[1] The Angles of 'Brittia' had no horses whatever and did not even know what a horse was! We need not accept this last point, but it is undoubtedly true that the Anglo-Saxon invaders of Britain can have brought few horses with them.[2] And it may well be the case that the only Germanic peoples of the sixth century A.D. whose main arm was cavalry, were the peoples who founded kingdoms in Italy, Africa, and Spain.[3]

In the sixth century, then, methods of warfare in the Mediterranean were far from standardized. The military methods of the Franks, of the Germans of the Mediterranean kingdoms, of the Byzantines, and of the Persians (to say nothing of the Slavs and the nomads of the steppe and the desert) all differed from one another; and it cannot reasonably be doubted that in normal conditions the equipment and tactics of the Byzantines, allied to the military skill and traditions of their commanders, were far superior to all the others. As an historical curiosity we may draw attention to the one recorded encounter of the Goths with the Persians. Belisarius had a number of Ostrogoths with him when he invaded the Persian Empire in 541, and when these

[1] Procopius, *BG* viii. 20. 31.
[2] Ibid., 28 f.; cf. H. M. Chadwick, *The Origin of the English Nation* (Cambridge, 1907), 150 n. 1.
[3] C. Oman, *A History of the Art of War* (London, 1898), 42, suggests that 'all the tribes which had their original habitat in the plains beyond the Danube and north of the Euxine seem to have learned horsemanship . . . The races, on the other hand, which had started from the marshes of the Lower Rhine or the moors of North Germany and Scandinavia were essentially foot-soldiers.'

charged a Persian force outside Nisibis, we are told, the Persians took to flight, unable to withstand the Ostrogoths who came at them with a dense array of long spears. But it would be rash to generalize from one skirmish and to conclude that Gothic methods of warfare were superior to those of the Persian Empire.[1]

However that may be, it seems reasonable to infer from our discussion that an army of German warriors, in the first century A.D. as in the sixth, could not hope to win a victory over a Roman army unless (a) it greatly outnumbered it, or (b) it was powerfully helped by the terrain, or (c) the Roman commander was as incompetent as Quintilius Varus was in the Teutoberg Forest or as the Emperor Valens was at Adrianople.

## 2. Siege Warfare

The more elaborate Roman weapons could not be made or used successfully by the northern barbarians owing to the low technical level of their society generally. Thus, the Batavians supplied considerable numbers of men to the Imperial forces; and their turbulent, unreliable behaviour coupled with their considerable military value, were a constant source of anxiety to their Roman paymasters.[2] Yet as late as A.D. 69, many years after they are first known to have served with the Romans,[3] the Batavians were utterly taken aback by at least one Roman military contrivance, the *tolleno*.[4]

Those who propose to destroy an urban civilization must be skilled in siege war; and sieges were not un-

[1] Procopius, *BP* ii. 18. 24.

[2] Tacitus, *H* i. 59, 64, ii. 27 f., 66, 69. On their political relations with Rome see J. Klose, *Roms Klientel-Randstaaten am Rhein und an der Donau* (Breslau, 1934), 17–26.

[3] Tacitus, *A* ii. 8. 3, 11. 3, shows them serving with the Imperial forces in A.D. 16.

[4] Id., *H* iv. 30.

known in conflicts between the free Germans living beyond the Imperial frontiers.[1] Little detailed information has survived to throw light upon their nature, but they certainly presented different problems from those raised when Germans attempted to besiege the walled cities and fortresses of the Empire. In the Roman opinion, however, the Germans were utterly unskilled in conducting sieges.[2] As we have said, the siege engines which the Romans regarded as absolutely essential[3] were too elaborate for them to make, and their lack of these and of defensive armour put them at a disastrous disadvantage when assailing the walls of a Roman town.[4] Even if they captured somewhat complicated weapons from the Romans or had them constructed by Roman prisoners or deserters, it was beyond their powers to work them in the absence of careful instruction and long practice. Thus, when the Batavians besieged Vetera in A.D. 69 some deserters and prisoners showed them how to make various siege engines;[5] but the ungainly contraptions which resulted from their efforts never even went into action, for they were easily smashed up by the artillery of the defending Romans.[6] And yet the Batavians, owing to their familiarity with Roman army service, were thought to be more proficient with such

[1] Tacitus, *A* i. 57. 1, xii. 29. 4. Germans besieged by Romans: Amm. Marc., xvii. 2; Priscus of Panium, frag. 1*a*; Agathias, i. 9; and the vivid picture on section liv of the Column of M. Aurelius (now reproduced in C. Caprino and others, *La Colonna di Marco Aurelio* (Rome, 1955), Plate xxxiv, fig. 68), where the German defenders of a fort throw swords (!), torches, and a jar of an unspecified liquid at a Roman *testudo*.

[2] Dio Cassius, lvi. 22. 2 ( =Zonaras, x. 37); Amm. Marc., xvii. 6. 1, xxix. 6. 12, etc. The Romans rarely admit that any barbarian people was efficient at siege-warfare.

[3] See e.g. Tacitus, *H* iii. 20.

[4] Ibid., ii. 22.

[5] Ibid., iv. 23. For the Jews note Josephus, *BJ* v. 268, 359.

[6] Tacitus, *H* loc. cit.; cf. 30 *init.*

machines than the Germans who lived in freedom beyond the Rhine outside the Roman frontier.[1]

Some of these free Germans could achieve even less than the Batavians. It is true that at the siege of Thessalonica in 269 the Gothic attackers are said to have used 'engines'; but there is no detailed information about these engines—except that the defenders countered them by hurling blazing missiles at them from their own artillery—and we cannot lightly assume that the Gothic engines were made by the Goths themselves rather than by Roman prisoners or deserters.[2] Siege engines are also said to have been used by the barbarians from beyond the Rhine—either Franks or Alamanni—when they besieged Tours during the reign of Postumus. A report reached the Eastern Empire some years later that when the defenders attacked these engines with some success by means of burning missiles the barbarians dug tanks to hold water behind their threatened engines, and filled these tanks with water. But how they used it to quench the fires started by the Romans is not recorded, for the fragmentary text of our authority breaks off at this point with a reference to lead-covered channels which would receive the water. But clearly, there is nothing here to suggest a high level of siege-craft on the part of the Germans.[3] Moreover, at the siege of Philippopolis in the middle of the century, we are told, the Goths put some warriors in large wooden boxes or crates, the size of a small room, covered with hides to keep off the enemy's missiles, and moved them on wheels to the city gates (where the

[1] Ibid., iv. 28.
[2] Eusebius, 101 F 2 § 2 (Jacoby).
[3] Eusebius, ibid., § 5, with P. Goessler, 'Zur Belagerungskunst der Germanen', *Klio*, xxxv (1942), 103–14, who in my opinion fails to prove the existence of a high siege-technique among the Germans.

citizens dropped huge stones on them and crushed both boxes and men).[1] Again, when they were besieging Side in Lycia *c*. 269, the Goths built towers of the same height as the city walls and moved them forward on wheels. They hung iron plates as well as hides in front of them so as to prevent the enemy from setting them on fire. But even so their attack came to nothing.[2] These boxes and towers and a mound of earth and wood (which they built so as to be able to fight on a level with the defenders of Philippopolis)[3] are practically the only siege-works which the barbarians are reported to have built during the third-century invasions. There is little doubt that the invaders had the ability to make all these contrivances, but we find a different state of affairs when we come to examine the attack by Goths and others on Marcianople in 248. The city was well stocked with food, and the barbarians did not propose to besiege it for they believed that it could be taken by storm. Their first move was to collect as many stones as possible from the ground round about the city and to pile them in convenient heaps in front of the city wall. They then surrounded the wall and began hurling these stones together with their spears and arrows at the defenders.[4] But the citizens behind their battlements merely held their shields over their heads, and the stones, spears, and arrows rattled and bounced off them like a heavy shower of hailstones. After a while all the stones and all the other missiles had been shot away,

[1] Dexippus, 100 F 27 (Jacoby).

[2] Dexippus, 100 F 29 (Jacoby). They had made wooden towers at Philippopolis also, id., F 27 § 5, but they had been burned by the defenders. Others, which were also burned, are mentioned in Eusebius, 101 F 2 § 5 (Jacoby), as belonging to the Franks or Alamanni.

[3] Dexippus, F 27 §§ 7–11.

[4] Cf. Tacitus, *H* v. 17 f. 'saxis glandibusque et ceteris missilibus proelium incipitur . . . absumptis quae iaciuntur', etc.

and little or no damage had been done to the defenders. The attackers went despondently away and encamped a short distance from the city. After a few days, which they may have spent in making new spears and arrows and in collecting more stones,[1] they returned and began the process all over again. But the citizens, whose courage was high and who had no lack of weapons, launched such a storm of missiles on the carelessly massed barbarians that they inflicted considerable losses upon them, broke their spirit, and convinced them that the attack was futile.[2] There is no trace here of boxes, towers, mounds, and the like, nor is there any trace of them among the fourth-century Visigoths. These found it exceedingly difficult to take the Roman cities by siege or by storm; and competent Roman observers held that the Visigoths knew nothing whatever of siege-craft.[3] Fritigern was quick to dissuade his men in 376 from sieges, 'saying that he was at peace with walls'. Occasionally, in fact, they forgot his advice, but each time they did so they met with so sharp a reverse as to recall his wise words without delay.[4] And in this incompetence they did not differ from the contemporary Alamanni.[5] Even in the late fifth century, when they beleaguered Clermont, they made no attempt to storm the town: they simply blockaded it, destroying the crops each year and then returning home for the winter. But there

[1] Cf. Procopius, *BG* vii. 24. 22.

[2] Dexippus, 100 F 25 (Jacoby).

[3] Amm. Marc., xxxi. 6. 4 'homines ignaros obsidendi', 8. 1 'haec et similia machinari penitus ignorantes', cf. 16. 3. The cities which survived the Visigothic invasions were in general the cities that were walled: Eunapius, frag. 42 (p. 240, 21. ed. Dindorf).

[4] Amm. Marc., xxxi. 6. 4; cf. Ambrose, *Ep.* xv. 5 and 7 (Migne, *PL* xvi. 997 f.); Zosimus, v. 19. 6.

[5] After they had besieged Julian in Sens for 30 days in 356, according to Amm. Marc., xvi. 4. 2, 'the barbarians went away sadly, grumbling about how silly it was to attempt sieges'.

is no evidence of any development of military technique beyond what had been known to their ancestors in Fritigern's day.[1]

The towers, boxes, mounds, etc., mentioned by Dexippus and Eusebius Historicus in the third century, then, if they are to be accepted as historical—and sometimes the accounts of sieges in late Greek historians are open to considerable doubt[2]—left little mark on the siege-craft of the invaders in general. We may suppose that some, but not all, of the groups of third-century invaders were able to make such contrivances; but such contrivances did not become part of the stock-in-trade of the northern barbarians in general. Indeed, they were forgotten by the Goths themselves before very long, for there is no parallel to them in Gothic history before the sixth century. The ability to make such things was temporary and it was local, being beyond the powers of some of the Goths themselves in the mid-third century. It may not be unreasonable to conclude that the siege of Marcianople in 248 was a much more typical siege than those of Philippopolis and Side. While the barbarians were more at home in taking unwalled cities,[3] it is of course true that a number of walled cities are reported to have been taken by them in the course of their raids and invasions; and it must not be supposed that protracted, vigorous, and sometimes successful sieges were unknown.[4] But few trustworthy details are available about the ways in which they took

[1] The siege of Clermont is well characterized by C. E. Stevens, *Sidonius Apollinaris and his Age* (Oxford, 1933), 145 ff., where the evidence is cited and discussed.

[2] E. A. Thompson, *Classical Quarterly*, xxxix (1945), 92-4.

[3] Zosimus, i. 26. 1, 33. 2, 43. 2, v. 19. 6; Syncellus, p. 382, Bonn.

[4] e.g. Amm. Marc., xv. 8. 19; Zosimus, i. 43. 1 (barbarian siege engines); Jordanes, *Get.* xvi. 92, xvii. 94, xviii. 103, etc. For unsuccessful sieges see Zosimus, i. 29. 2, 32. 1, etc.

the walled cities and fortresses, and it is difficult to avoid the impression that they did so, not by prolonged siege, but by surprise or treachery or by the panic or incompetence or negligence of the defenders.[1]

The Germans of the sixth-century kingdoms can hardly be said to have advanced significantly in siege-warfare as compared with the Germans of earlier times. Thus, when Witigis beleaguered Rome in 536 he built some wooden towers equal in height to the city walls. These towers had a wheel at each corner, and oxen were yoked to them so as to draw the towers forward.[2] But the oxen were all promptly shot by Roman archers on the walls as soon as they came within range, and the towers became immobile; and Belisarius not unreasonably was able to laugh at the simplicity of the barbarians.[3] (He had travelled a long way since that day when on his way to Africa he had stepped ashore in Sicily under the shadow of Mount Etna, not knowing what manner of men the Vandals were or what kind of warfare they practised.)[4] The Ostrogoths were more successful when they tried simply to clear the walls of their defenders by firing at them an overwhelming number of arrows and without using any machines at all.[5] Witigis, however, still persisted in building 'engines' —for the barbarians never failed to grasp the value of engines if only they could be made to work—but all his constructions were set on fire and destroyed by Belisarius.[6]

The king made yet another attempt to solve his

---

[1] See e.g. Tacitus, *H* iv. 33; Dexippus, 100 F 28 § 5 (Jacoby); Zosimus, i. 33. 2, 34. 3, 35. 1, etc.
[2] Procopius, v. 21. 3 ff. Observe Witigis' four great battering-rams which were also mounted on wheels and moved by 50 men.
[3] Ibid., 22. 8 f.      [4] Id., *BV* iii. 14. 1.
[5] Id., *BG* v. 22. 19 ff.      [6] Ibid., 23. 17 and 23.

problem when he came to besiege Ariminum in 537–8. Once again he built a wooden tower—this time higher than the city walls—and once again he mounted it upon four wheels. But he did not repeat the mistake of yoking oxen to it, for in this respect he had learned his lesson at Rome. There was a very wide ladder inside the tower; and the king's aim was that his men should swarm up this ladder as soon as it came close enough to the city wall. On paper his plan was no doubt practicable, but his tactical handling of the tower was atrocious. His men drew it close to the wall, but then darkness fell and they were obliged to leave the tower all night close to the wall of Ariminum. During the night the Romans dug a trench in front of it, and next day despite considerable effort the Ostrogoths could not move the tower forward. Hence, afraid that the Romans would burn it during the following night, they pulled the tower back, and reached their camp with it late that day. In doing so, however, they suffered such severe casualties that they decided to assault the wall no more.[1] The tower was little more than a death-trap for its builders.

When Totila became king of the Ostrogoths he rarely besieged the Roman-held cities in an active manner: he merely blockaded them. But he pulled down the walls of cities which fell into his hands and which he feared might become centres of Roman resistance if Belisarius should manage to re-occupy them. This had been the policy of Geiseric in Africa,[2] and when the Visigoths recaptured Cartagena in Spain from the Byzantines *c.*

[1] Ibid., vi. 12. 1–13, 24 f.
[2] Id., *BV* iii. 5. 8, 15. 9, though note 16. 9. Striking confirmation of the historian has been found at Tipasa, where the city walls were systematically destroyed and the towers overturned: see J. Baradez, *Tipasa: Ville antique de Maurétanie* (Algiers, 1952), 69, with Plate 42. The African cities were re-fortified by Solomon in 539–40: Procopius, *BV* iv. 19. 3,

615 they laid it waste.[1] Witigis had initiated this policy of despair in the case of two only of the cities of Italy (Pisaurum and Fanum),[2] but it was Totila who applied it on an extensive scale.[3] He even planned at one time to level Rome itself with the ground. He did in fact do considerable damage to the city and left it wholly un-inhabited in 546–7; but he was afterwards criticized by the Ostrogothic nobles for not destroying the city com-pletely.[4] In the final chapter of Procopius' *Gothic War* we hear at last of the successful use of military machines by the Ostrogoths. They seized a bridge over the river Dracon or Sarnus (modern Sarno) near Nuceria, put wooden towers on it, and in these towers placed ballistae, which at long last they worked effectively.[5] But this case is exceptional.

Finally, a description has survived from the late seventh century of a Visigothic attack on two walled cities. When king Wamba was suppressing the great rebellion of Paulus and others in 673 he found it neces-sary to assault the cities of Narbonne and Nîmes. Our authority for the attacks makes no reference to the use of siege engines: the Goths threw stones and fired arrows and spears at the city walls just as their ancestors had done at Thessalonica 400 years before. But they did so to such effect that they were able to get close to the gates of both cities, set them on fire, and so make their way inside the walls.[6] Generally speaking, then, the

---

20. 29. Among other works Solomon built an extraordinarily impressive fort a short distance south of Timgad: C. Courtois, *Timgad: Antique Thamugadi* (Algiers, 1951), 60–6.

[1] Isidore, *Etymol.* xv. 1. 67; cf. Fredegarius, iv. 33.
[2] Procopius, *BG* vii. 11. 32, 25. 7.
[3] Ibid., vii. 6. 1, 25. 11 (Beneventum), 8. 10 (Naples), 23. 3 (Spoletium), 24. 32 f. (Tibur); cf. 24. 29.
[4] Ibid., 22. 6 ff., and 19; 24. 3, 9, and 27.  [5] Ibid., viii. 35. 9.
[6] Julianus, *Hist. Wambae* xii, xiii, xvii, xviii (*MGH, SS. rer. Merov.* v).

progress which the Ostrogoths and the Visigoths had made in the latest days of their kingdoms was very slight and marked only a small advance over the abilities of Fritigern or even Arminius.

Strong though the Roman military forces were in comparison with those of the barbarians, they were nowhere stronger than in siege warfare. Tacitus has been called the most unmilitary of historians, but he knew that the barbarians were nowhere weaker, and the Romans nowhere more powerful, than in the equipment and the tactics of a siege.[1]

### 3. Strategy and Food

When Constantius II heard that Julian had rebelled against him in Paris he arranged to have three million bushels of wheat distributed among the cities on the borders of Gaul, and a further three million bushels concentrated in the region of the Cottian Alps, so as to feed his army when he marched from the East to engage the rebel's forces.[2] The commissariat of the Imperial government was almost infinitely superior to anything that any northern people could hope to organize. When an army of northern barbarians undertook a campaign, its leaders did not think in terms of millions of bushels of wheat. They usually did not think of organizing food supplies at all, for it seems to have been each man's business to supply his own food; and the Chatti, who organized some sort of supply system, were regarded as exceptional and noteworthy.[3] Hence, as soon as the warriors assembled for the purpose of

---

[1] Tacitus, *A* xii. 45. 4. He never ascribes bows and arrows as weapons of war to the Germans.

[2] Julian, *Ep. ad Ath.* 286 B.

[3] Tacitus, *G* xxx. 3 *copiis.* Sometimes women would accompany German warriors so as to serve food, ibid., vii. 4.

undertaking a campaign, it was imperative to enter the enemy's territory as soon as possible, for one could not plunder the food of one's own people—plundering within one's own people's territory was a punishable offence.[1]

A campaign fought far from home meant that the warriors would have to live largely off the countryside which they overran.[2] Accordingly, one of the first measures which the Romans might take in a province where an invasion had begun or even where it still only threatened—and particularly if earlier raids had taught the population what to expect—was to drive all the livestock from the fields into the cities, to transport the grain to places of security, and to remove all possible sources of food supply out of reach of the ill-stocked raiders so as to hasten the famine which would soon demoralize and destroy them.[3] And then Roman strategy might aim, not at major engagements with the enemy and not necessarily even at a struggle with each and every one of their bands, but at starving them into surrender or flight.[4] If the Romans chose to reach an accommodation with the raiders before the bands of the latter had altogether disintegrated, the Imperial authorities might be obliged to supply the raiders with food-markets as they made their hungry way back to the frontier.[5] On the other hand, a cautious barbarian might refrain from charging wildly over the maximum extent

[1] Caesar, *BG* vi. 23. 6 *extra finis*; cf. *Legg. Visigoth.* viii. 1. 9; cf. Julianus, *Hist. Wambae* x, *Legg. Baiuvar.* ii. 5. But the Franks were very lax in this respect: see Dalton, op. cit. 227 ff.

[2] Note Caesar, *BG* ii. 10. 4.

[3] See e.g. Amm. Marc., xviii. 7. 3 f., xxxi. 8. 1; Vegetius, iv. 7; Libanius, *Or.* xxiv. 38; Zosimus, i. 43. 2 *fin.*, 48. 1, v. 19. 6 f. (cf. 21. 2); Eugippius, *Vita S. Severini* xxx. 2 (where note *statim*).

[4] Caesar, *BG* vi. 10. 2; *Paneg. Lat.* x (ii). 5. 2 (cf. *SHA, Claudius*, xi. 3); Amm. Marc., xxxi. 7. 3, 8. 1.

[5] Dexippus, 100 F 7 § 3 (Jacoby), cf. F. 6 § 14.

of Roman territory in search of plunder and might instead content himself with merely amassing enough supplies from the Roman countryside in his immediate neighbourhood to enable him to keep his army concentrated and organized until he could bring the Imperial forces to battle.[1] But it might often be well for him if no very long time elapsed before battle was joined.

The Visigothic campaigns on the lower Danube in 376 and the following years are an extreme illustration of the procedure of a Germanic host on entering the Roman provinces. The Visigoths had been starved by the Roman commanders on the Danube in 376 who admitted them to the Empire, which they entered without any food supplies at all. They proceeded to split up into comparatively small companies (which could be more easily fed than one large host), and guided by dissident Romans they kept constantly on the move from one source of supply to another, from villa to villa, from granary to granary.[2] The war became one of 'flights and pursuits', as a contemporary put it.[3] Such a strategy gave the invaders several advantages (p. 146 below), particularly as they could rapidly re-assemble their foraging parties whenever danger threatened.[4] But the risk was that these small parties might be cut off and destroyed one by one. In the early summer months of 378 the general Sebastian, whom some regarded as the most able Roman soldier of his day and who had not been without a chance of succeeding Valentinian I as

---

[1] Id., F 6 § 5; cf. Caesar, *BG* i. 34. 3.
[2] Amm. Marc., xxxi. 7. 6 and 8 *necessitas*. Their small bands are mentioned repeatedly: ibid., 5. 8, 6. 5, 7. 7, 9. 3, 10. 21, 11. 4 and 5; cf. *SHA, Aurelian* xviii. 6; Claudian, *In Rufin.* ii. 124 f.; and many similar phrases.
[3] Libanius, *Or.* xxiv. 40.     [4] Claudian, loc. cit.

Emperor,[1] eventually organized a troop of 2,000 specially picked and trained soldiers to hunt them down;[2] and we have more than one vivid picture of the surprise and shattering defeat of these small groups of Visigoths. After a good day's foraging and plundering in the fields and unfortified villages they would gorge themselves with what food they had found, and drink themselves to sleep; then an hour or two before dawn a watchful foe could sometimes kill them to a man as they lay and slept.[3] By these tactics of continuous harrying Sebastian hoped to prevent the Visigoths from collecting food and to compel them either to surrender to the Emperor or to withdraw north of the Danube: they would face the Huns north of the Danube rather than famine south of it.[4]

It might be thought, however, that the Visigoths were an exceptional case in 376–8 and that a generalization based on their experience would give a misleading picture of Germanic invasions and raids in general. The Visigoths had been driven abruptly from their homes by the Huns, and the Romans had robbed them of whatever small stocks of food they had been able to snatch up and carry with them as they fled in panic from their country. Moreover, it was not simply a fighting force which entered the provinces in 376: they brought their womenfolk and their children with them.

And yet in their third-century raids, which presumably were planned with some care, the later stages of an expedition might see the Goths starving, and the men and pack-animals dying off from hunger or

---

[1] Amm. Marc., xxx. 10. 3.
[2] Id., xxxi. 11. 2–5; Eunapius, frag. 47; Zosimus, iv. 23.
[3] Zosimus, iv. 25. 3 f.; cf. 23. 4; Amm. Marc., xxxi. 11. 4.
[4] Zosimus, iv. 23. 6. See Eunapius, frag. 47, for a panegyric of Sebastian.

succumbing a little later to plague and sickness.[1] It may be doubted whether many German invasions of the Roman Empire were preceded by two years of preparation and by a deliberate and planned extension of the area under crops, like the Helvetic movement of 58 B.C.[2] And when we turn to the other accounts of the invasions we find that although the case of the Visigoths in 376 was extreme it was not qualitatively different from the general experience. When Gaul was invaded by the Alamanni in the middle of the fourth century the invaders had chosen their own time for the attack. Their homes were close in their rear. Their economy produced a surplus of food over and above the bare essential needed to keep them alive, so that in theory at any rate it might have been possible to organize a commissariat: and since in 354 and 355 there was little or no organized Roman opposition—the Roman generals in the neighbourhood, according to one authority, had chosen to fall asleep[3]— any supply trains that the Alamanni could have put on the roads would for the most part have reached their warriors in Gaul practically unmolested. Yet in spite of all these advantages the fate of the Alamannic invaders was not very different from that of the Visigoths in 376. Soon after Julian's arrival in Gaul at the end of 355 he found that the invaders were desperate for food. They were not living on what they had brought from their homes but on whatever food they could collect from the countryside which they were invading. They made for the flocks and herds of the provincials without any

[1] Zosimus, i. 45. 1, 46. 1; *SHA, Claudius* xi. 3, xii. 1. On their scattered bands see Dexippus, 100 F 26 § 3, 28 § 1.

[2] Caesar, *BG* i. 3. 1 f.

[3] Amm. Marc., xv. 8. 1, xvi. 12. 5; Libanius, *Or.* xviii. 42. So, too, there seems to have been little organized opposition to the Visigoths when Theodosius became Emperor at the beginning of 379: Themistius, *Or.* xvi. 207 AB.

regard for their own safety, so great was their hunger. But this food was soon gone, and in many cases Julian actually found that they were dying of hunger before they could collect more.[1] When a district had often been ravaged thus, as in 354–5, it was reduced to a wilderness, and practically no food at all could be extracted from it either by invader or by native Roman: the crops could not be sown or reaped.[2] Hence, again and again in the Alamannic invasions, at any rate after the initial stages, the warriors divided up into a number of mere 'plundering bands' living off the country: they were no longer one united and centrally directed army. This was generally the case throughout Julian's years in Gaul, and again during the reign of Valentinian I, the two periods for which detailed information exists.[3] As for the numbers of men in such bands, Julian considered that several parties of Franks, amounting in all to 600 warriors, formed very strong companies.[4] It is no wonder that a military writer of the sixth century A.D., when discussing the best tactics to use against the Lombards and the Franks, states that it is essential to delay

[1] Amm. Marc., xvi. 5. 17. For a third-century Alamannic parallel see Dexippus, 100 F 6 § 14, and for the fifth century Eugippius, *Vita S. Severini* xxx. 4.

[2] Amm. Marc., xvi. 4. 4; *Paneg. Lat.* xi (iii). 15. 3; Zosimus, iii. 5. 1.

[3] Amm. Marc., xvi. 2. 2 'per diversa palantes barbaros', 7 'diffusae multitudinis barbarae', 11. 3 'vagantesque fusius', 12. 4, xxi. 3. 1, xxvii. 1. 1, 2. 1–2, 10. 4; cf. Libanius, *Or* xiii. 24. So also the Alamannic Lentienses in 378; Amm. Marc., xxxi. 10. 4. Julian expected the Alamanni to *begin* the campaign of 358 in one compact army (Amm. Marc., xvii. 8. 1 'Alamannos nondum in unum coactos'), but doubtless they would have divided up according to rule (and necessity) after a very few days.

[4] Id., xvii. 2. 1. An inferior authority (Libanius, *Or.* xviii. 70) speaks of 1,000 Franks on that same occasion. In 457 the Alamanni operating near Bellinzona numbered 900, Sidonius, *carm.* v. 377. But one of the Alamannic bands raiding Gaul in 366 is said to have consisted of at least 10,000 warriors (Amm. Marc., xxvii. 2. 7), though of course the figures of enemy killed and wounded are frequently exaggerated.

joining battle with them: time must be wasted by opening sham negotiations with them, for then their courage and enthusiasm will be sapped by the failure of their supplies and by their exposure to the severe climate of the South.[1]

The position of the invaders, broken up into a multiplicity of small parties, was not in all respects one of weakness. When the Roman defensive was totally disorganized, as it was in Gaul in 355, these bands of Alamanni, roving over enormous areas of the province, penetrating everywhere, and making their appearance at unexpected places without warning, could reduce a countryside to chaos. We are told that the inhabitants would shrink away at the very mention of the barbarians;[2] and a contemporary writer refers to the raids as 'an Iliad of misfortunes'.[3] It was exceedingly difficult for the Romans to move small detachments of their troops with any feeling of security, for in the general confusion they could not foresee at what moment the troops might be surprised and cut to pieces, when every road and every bridge might conceal an ambush.[4] Thus, during his first campaign in Gaul in June 356, Julian set out from Vienne to Autun 'intending to attack the barbarians, who were wandering over various districts, wherever chance should give him an opportunity'.[5] And the events of his march showed that he had no idea whatever of where the barbarian bands

[1] Mauricius, *Strateg.* xi. 4, p. 271, ed. Scheffer. So, too, Agathias, *Hist.* i. 19.

[2] Zosimus, iii. 3. 2.

[3] Libanius, *Or.* lix. 136. The phrase, which is proverbial (cf. Demosthenes, *Or.* xix. 148, etc.), is used by Themistius, *Or.* xvi. 216 D, of the Visigothic raids after 376.

[4] Amm. Marc., xvi. 2. 11. See xvi. 2, and Libanius, *Or.* xviii. 35, for vivid pictures of the disorganization of Gaul in 355 and the difficulties of fighting in such conditions.

[5] Amm. Marc., xvi. 2. 2.

lay, except that they were lurking in the woods close beside him. Such ignorance of the enemy's whereabouts and of the character of his forces might cause a serious waste not only of time but also of food and weapons.[1] Again, just before his victory at Strasbourg in 357 Julian was reluctant to join battle with the Alamanni because his own men were tired after a long march. But when he suggested postponing the engagement, his men protested on the ground that *the enemy were now before their eyes*. Julian's staff officers, while recognizing the risks of an immediate battle, urged the Caesar to attack at once when the Alamanni were concentrated. They declared that the troops might well mutiny if the barbarians were permitted to disperse again, and the Romans were faced with the hazardous and endless task of rounding up innumerable elusive parties of the foe.[2] Even under the strong rule of Valentinian I, an able Imperial general named Dagalaifus long refrained from trying to repel the Alamannic invasion of 365; he pleaded that it was impossible for him to attack the enemy while they were scattered in small bands over a wide area. He was less enterprising, however, than his successor Jovinus, who early in 366 managed to surprise the three main bodies of the enemy who had daunted Dagalaifus. Jovinus caught and dispersed one of these bodies after they had plundered some of the villas in the Moselle valley and were now resting in their 'robbers' camp' beside the river. Some were bathing, some drinking, some dyeing their hair red, when the Romans burst out of the shelter of some neighbouring trees and fell upon them.[3] It is difficult, then, to avoid the impression

[1] *SHA, Aurelian*, xi. 6.
[2] Amm. Marc., xvi. 12. 13 f. Contrast P. Ostorius' attitude in Tacitus, *A* xii. 31. 2 'ne rursus conglobarentur'.
[3] Amm. Marc., xxvii. 2. 1–3.

that Chonodomarius made a grave mistake in assembling all the Alamannic forces at Strasbourg in 357 and in risking a general engagement with the Imperial army, even though he outnumbered it. He was doubtless encouraged to risk open battle by his earlier success against Barbatio and a Roman army of 25,000 men, but he forgot that that victory was due to surprise.[1] The curious fact in late Roman history is not that the Romans lost or won so few pitched battles, but rather that the barbarians allowed large-scale battles to take place at all.[2] But even when the enemy had dispersed, the Romans often found little difficulty in working out methods of eliminating their lightly equipped raiding parties. A fourth-century author says that one Emperor, when marching against the Germans, 'brought with him Eastern auxiliaries chiefly for the reason that no troops are more effective against Germans than light-armed archers', and the truth of this opinion was widely recognized in the days when Germanic levies consisted mainly of unmounted warriors.[3] If the Imperial forces could not simply starve the enemy into surrender, their best course was to lay ambushes continuously for the scattered bands of the enemy, to make lightning sallies, to cut off their supplies, and to score a very quick succession of victories over their foraging parties. This was what Sebastian did in the year or two preceding the

---

[1] Id., xv. 4. 8. For a similar mistake see xxvii. 2. 4 ff.

[2] In the opinion of Strabo, iv. 4. 2, the reason why the Gauls, unlike the Iberians, had been crushed so quickly by Rome was the fact that they concentrated their forces and fought pitched battles. The Germans would have done well to ponder Livy, iii. 2. 12 f.

[3] *SHA*, *Maximinus* xi. 8; cf. *Aurelian* xi. 3; Herodian, *Hist.* vi. 7. 8, vii. 2. 2; John of Antioch, frag. 141. 1; Eunapius, frag. 42 (p. 240. 29, ed. Dindorf); Zosimus, iv. 22. 1–3; and the criticism of Julian in Amm. Marc., xvi. 2. 6. Moors were similarly used by Belisarius; Procopius, *BG* v. 29. 22; cf. 25. 9, vi. 23. 36.

battle of Adrianople.[1] This was how Charietto helped
Julian to overwhelm the Chamavian Franks in 358.[2]
This procedure was useful when the enemy could not be
brought to a general engagement or when the terrain
made it impossible to attack them in any other way.[3] It
is not unfair to conclude that in a campaign against the
Romans (as distinct from a battle) a Germanic chief
could only hope to win if he were, like Caratacus, able
to exploit skilfully his knowledge of the terrain[4] or if the
Roman commander was as incompetent as Quintilius
Varus or Valens.

[1] Zosimus, iv. 23. 4. Note also Dexippus, 100 F 28 § 1 (Jacoby); Amm.
Marc., xxxi. 7. 3.

[2] Zosimus, iii. 7. 1–3; Eunapius, frag. 11; cf. Amm. Marc., xvii. 10. 5,
xxvii. 1.

[3] Id., xxxi. 7. 2; Eunapius, frag. 46.     [4] Tacitus, A xii. 33. 2.

# EPILOGUE

What happened after the events described by Tacitus? We can hardly be said to know. Sources of information are almost wholly lacking apart from some details, valuable but disconnected, given by Dio Cassius and one or two others. Internal German history during the second and third centuries and the first half of the fourth is exceedingly obscure. These centuries are the Dark Age of the continental Germans. We can draw no clear picture, not even a dim outline, of the development of German society between the close of Tacitus' *Annals* and the beginning, in 353, of the extant part of the narrative of Ammianus Marcellinus. This is all the more regrettable because German society, as is clear from what we have seen, was moving towards a crisis in Tacitus' day, and the later stages of that crisis, and its outcome, cannot now be discovered.

When at last Ammianus throws light on conditions in western Germany the landscape has changed. The peoples of western Germany, whom Tacitus described, have in most cases disappeared from history. The Cherusci, the Chatti, and the others are no longer prominent: they scarcely seem to exist at all. Instead, the country is now filled by the new confederacies of the Alamanni south of the river Main, the Franks north of it, and the Burgundians behind them, while on the seacoast live the Saxons. Not one of these peoples had been known to Tacitus, at any rate under those names.

What, then, had happened in the meantime? Whether these new peoples were formed by immigrants from the east or whether they are simply re-groupings of

the earlier peoples is unknown. Certainly, vast move-
ments of peoples took place in the obscure centuries.
Between 150 and 200, for example, the Goths left their
homes on the lower Vistula, where Tacitus had known
of their presence, and moved to the shores of the Black
Sea. But it does not necessarily follow that the Alamanni
and the Burgundians had also moved from the remote
east to the neighbourhood of the Rhine, though they
may have done so.

Where nothing is certain, a guess may be risked. We
have seen earlier that some of the peoples of western
Germany were in a state of rapid development when
Tacitus was writing. Tensions between the optimates
and the rank-and-file warriors, which had scarcely
existed in the time of Julius Caesar, were now acute. In
the case of the Cherusci they had become so intense and
so destructive that the entire people had lost its military
power and had sunk into insignificance (p. 88 above).
We may guess that the same thing happened among
most of the major peoples who crowd the pages of the
*Germania*. Internal warfare between all or some of the
tribal nobility and their supporters, on the one hand,
and the common warriors on the other, may well have
ruined them, as it had ruined the Cherusci, and may
thus have cleared the stage for new groupings and a new
political scene. But whether mass immigration from
eastern Germany further confused the countryside is
not at present certain.

What is clear is that the internal organization of the
new confederacies was remarkably similar to that
described by Tacitus. The institutions changed but
little. The chief is still *primus inter pares*: even Alaric the
Goth wields influence rather than power, and an autocratic prince like Maroboduus is as hard to find in the

fourth century as in the first. Methods of warfare have undergone no major change apart from the extension of the use of bows and arrows as weapons of war. It is still impossible to hold down a defeated enemy and exploit him as a subject. Law codes and formal law courts, whose decisions are enforced by police and by a standing army, are still in the future; and so on. Drastic change first took place when the Visigoths and Burgundians established their kingdoms in Gaul. In the pages of Ammianus, however, the peoples' names have changed since Tacitus' day, but not much else.

# INDEX

Adgandestrius, chief of Chatti, 83

Adiatunnus of Aquitania, 55

Adrianople, battle of, 116 f., 118, 119, 131, 149

Aetius, 125

African slavery, 25

Agathias on German weapons, 113 f.

Agriculture, 17; contempt for, 53; importance of, 4 f., 26 f.; improvement of, 26 f.

Ahenobarbus, L. Domitius, 77

Aioulfus, a Visigoth, 96 n. 3

Aistomodius, Septimius, tombstone of, 101 n. 1

Alamanni, 150 f.; at Bellinzona, 145 n. 4; chieftainship among, 13 n. 2, 14; its complexity, 40; chiefs overruled, 46 n. 1; defeat at Strasbourg, 147; inefficiency in siege-warfare, 135; in fourth century, 144 ff.; invade Gaul in third century, 145 n. 1; land-tenure among, 18 n. 2; *regalis* of, 40 n. 3; Tours besieged by, 133, cf. 134 n. 2; warfare of, 64 n.1, 118

Alans, 117, 118 n. 1

Alaric, 151

Amber, 24

Ampsivarii, 78, 106

Angles, 130

*ango*, 129 n. 4

Ansgar, Saint, 25 n. 2

Antae, 113 n. 1

Antoninus Pius, Emperor, 94 n. 1

Aquitania, 55 f.

Arable, allocation of, 8, 10 f.; Caesar's comment on, 9 f.; individual use of in Tacitus'

time, 18, 25 f.; value increases in first century, 27. See also Land

Archers, 148 (Oriental); Ostrogothic, 121 ff., 127, 137; Persian, 122; Roman, 121 ff. See also Bows

Ariminum, siege of, 138

Ariogaisus, chieftain of Quadi, 102

Ariovistus, marries a Celt, 59; negotiations of, 14 f.; powers of, 95; his *vectigalia*, 70 n. 3

Aristus, Roman general, 110, 120

Arminius, son of Sigimer, 34 n. 2, 72; marries Thusnelda, 79 n. 2; chief at age of 26, 29, 72, 79; serves with Romans, 72 f.; imprisoned by Segestes, 37; imprisons Boiocalus, 78; destroys Quintilius Varus, 73; organizes resistance to Germanicus, 43; quarrels with Segestes, 79; overruled by Cherusci in A.D. 15, 37; attacks Marcomanni in A.D. 17, 65 f., 82 f.; aims at tyranny, 83 f.; limited powers of, 37 n. 3; death of, 84; 'the liberator of Germany', 83

Artabanus, 102 n. 1

Assembly of warriors, 12 n. 2, 15, 41 ff.; business of, 31, 46 f.; business pre-considered by *principes*, 31; elects judges, 61 f.; judicial functions of, 46 f., 62; need for initiative of *principes*, 31, 93; retinues' independence from, 55 f.; *rex* and, 35; Romans interfere with, 103

153

# INDEX

PRINTED IN GREAT BRITAIN BY ROBERT MACLEHOSE AND CO. LTD
THE UNIVERSITY PRESS, GLASGOW